WELCOME
HOME

How stuff makes or breaks
your relationship

SUZANNE ROYNON

Welcome Home

First published in 2020 by

Panoma Press Ltd
48 St Vincent Drive, St Albans, Herts, AL1 5SJ, UK
info@panomapress.com
www.panomapress.com

Book layout by Neil Coe.

978-1-784529-12-3

The right of Suzanne Roynon to be identified as the author of this work has been asserted in accordance with sections 77 and 78 of the Copyright, Designs and Patents Act 1988.

A CIP catalogue record for this book is available from the British Library.

This book is available online and in bookstores.

DEDICATION

For

Antonia and Vanessa

You each inspire me more than words can say

ACKNOWLEDGEMENTS

I express my immense gratitude to the following amazing people who gifted their time, encouragement and wisdom along the way to help this book from laptop to publication.

Russell Beck

Vanessa Edwards

Helen Fox

Mindy Gibbins-Klein

Andy Harrington

Adele-Marie Hartshorn

Michael Higgs

Annie Hunt

Antonia Hunter

Dr Steve G Jones

Cosmo Landesman

Zareh Langridge

Nathalie Le Mao

Frances Newman

Elizabeth Pickering

Marcia Roberts

Louise K Shaw

Catherine Waller

PREFACE

This book is based on nine fundamental truths:

1.   The older you are, the more history you carry.

2.   Your history and experience influence your response to every situation.

3.   The debris you carry in the form of physical and emotional 'stuff' makes it difficult to create space for something new.

4.   Memories in the form of possessions encourage your subconscious to repeat old patterns in relationships. Different person, same experience.

5.   By using Interiors Therapy for your home, you gain clarity on what's holding you back.

6.   Understanding how your clutter impacts your life leads to a change in perspective.

7.   By clearing physically and emotionally using the principles of Interiors Therapy, you change your thinking.

8.   By consolidating Interiors Therapy, new positive energy can reach you.

9.   By choosing to take action, you have the option to create the lifestyle you want.

CONTENTS

INTRODUCTION

This book is for you if you:

- ❤ tolerate unhappy relationships rather than be alone

- ❤ just settle for someone

- ❤ bounce from one unsatisfactory relationship to the next

- ❤ seem to experience the same relationship over and again with different people

- ❤ believe the last chance for love has gone

- ❤ accept a partner under family pressure

- ❤ choose to be alone because it's easier that way

You might have experienced a number of those situations or just one. Whatever your circumstances, you are here now, dipping into this book and wondering whether this is going to be the catalyst to something infinitely better.

So if I show you how the possessions (not just the clutter!) you keep around you can have a negative and soul-destroying impact on any romance, and can also cause:

- ❤ Poor health

- ❤ Depression

- ❤ Anxiety

- ❤ Weight gain

- ❤ Tiredness and exhaustion

- ❤ Stress and overwhelm

❤ Reduced productivity

❤ And a whole lot more…

Would you agree it might be time to do something about it?

Excellent, because that's what this book will help you do.

When is the best time to begin my Interiors Therapy?

One of the questions I often get asked at talks and workshops is, *"How do I know I need Interiors Therapy?"*

Essentially, if you are living your dream life, you are happy, healthy, have the money you need to pay your bills and enjoy yourself; your work, passions, travel and all your relationships are going well and you are thriving, then your home is supporting you every step of the way and you can probably hold off on your Interiors Therapy for a while!

If however, any of those issues raised earlier in this introduction feel uncomfortably familiar, then Interiors Therapy is long overdue, and it's definitely the best time to start!

❤ If you are ready to make a significant change in your life.

❤ If things aren't going well at home, at work, within your family or romantic relationships.

❤ If you don't have a relationship and would like to meet someone who really suits you.

❤ If you are stressed, overwhelmed, anxious or generally dissatisfied with your situation.

❤ If you feel constantly drained, exhausted or are barely coping with your daily existence.

❤ If you feel trapped or stagnant.

❤ If you are frustrated because, regardless of the action you take, something always gets in your way.

❤ If you are ready to move on from a failing relationship there is absolutely no point in packing up everything you own and taking it with you – all you do is transfer the problem into your new life. Deal with it first and then go.

❤ If your partner has moved out, leaving you lost and broken hearted.

❤ If you have reached the point in a grieving process where you are ready to look ahead instead of living in the past.

❤ If your health and wellbeing aren't as good as you'd like them to be.

❤ If you feel constantly aggrieved, unhappy, bored, unappreciated and basically miserable.

❤ If you feel you just have too much stuff.

❤ If some parts of your life are going really well and others just stink.

❤ If someone who cares about you has gifted you this book.

These are all excellent reasons to get started on your Interiors Therapy without delay.

So why has it taken so long for this book to find its way to you?

Interiors Therapy for relationships has been brewing for 17 years. "Seventeen years?" I can hear you saying, "That's procrastination on a grand scale."

Well yes and no, I like to see it as being nurtured, tested, reviewed, and ultimately born to create a positive niche in a world where vast negativity currently abounds.

Interiors Therapy is just one part of making life work for you, but for many of the people I've worked with over the years, it is the key change to making the biggest difference. People who believed themselves to be permanently single or spent years and many thousands of pounds in therapy, as well as individuals who were barely coping financially, now thrive after changing the physical and emotional energy around them.

Like all the best things in life, in order to get the true benefit of Interiors Therapy, you have to invest time and effort into the process and, I can't say this often enough, you have to follow through.

It's ridiculously easy to have a quick win at the beginning of the process and assume you've done everything you need to do.

As Julia Roberts says in *Pretty Woman,*

"Big Mistake. Big. Huge!"

Just as you can't expect to be a competent driver after learning how to switch on the ignition, gaining real benefit from Interiors Therapy means engaging with it throughout your home, and ultimately, you'll find you extend the impact into other areas of your life. If you go into it with half measures or give up after doing a little bit of de-cluttering, you're likely to be disappointed, and that would be sad for me as well as you.

The initial plan for this book was to focus on using one element of the Interiors Therapy process, the 'Manifesto for Love™' to open up your life and your home to a loving, kind, generous and wonderful relationship.

What became clear as the book was being written is that sharing just one part of a much wider concept would do you, my amazing reader, an injustice.

You need, and deserve, to go a whole lot deeper because right now, your emotional health, your self-esteem and your future happiness depend on it.

So the book is written in three parts. Each is individually crafted to get you on track to a happier, more personally fulfilling life and, if you so choose, a relationship genuinely worthy of the person you become.

I strongly recommend following the process rather than cherry-picking the bits you fancy!

So how is this going to work?

Part 1 is designed to get to grips with your situation right now and identify what is holding you back. It's going to start the process of shifting your emotional energy and attitude. This is fundamental to reprogramming your internal sat-nav to point you in the right direction.

Part 2 focuses on the basics of Interiors Therapy, taking a close look at the past and present of the possessions and memories you keep around you.

If we continue the car analogy, it's the equivalent of having a super-intense service and valet of your vehicle, so it runs brilliantly and feels fresh and new. And as any driver will know, a car always runs better after a skilled mechanic has tuned it up.

Part 3 is the blueprint for creating your Manifesto for Love™. While it may be tempting to skip forward, if you choose to jump ahead without building firm foundations first, you are doing yourself, and any potential romance, a disservice. This is where we put the fuel in the car and your foot on the accelerator, and you aim for the open road with nothing in your way.

It doesn't matter who you are, where you come from or what you do, by making you think about everything you keep around you then we can work together to make the change you want happen... and that's why you're really here.

CHAPTER 1

Where are you now?

So let's get started by understanding what you actually want to get out of this book.

You have realised whatever you have done so far hasn't panned out… perhaps your marriage or partnership isn't as happy as you'd like it to be; maybe you've had a series of unsatisfactory relationships, or you are back 'out there' in the dating game looking for new love after the end of something really special.

Wherever you are at, it's daunting, scary, potentially very alien, and if you've made mistakes or been treated badly, meeting someone who is genuinely right for you might seem impossible.

I'm here to point you in the right direction and assure you that somewhere out there in our world of billions of people, there are many people who would love and cherish being in a long term romantic relationship with you… and you have the potential to feel exactly the same about one or more of them.

All you have to do is decide exactly what you want, get yourself into the best possible place physically, emotionally, mentally and practically, and the world is your oyster – simple!

"No!" you're shouting – it's not simple; if it were we would all be living our 'happily ever after' with Prince or Princess Charming and life would be easy.

Ok, whoa there, stay with me. As my good friend and dating coach Miia Koponen says,

Happy ever after does not exist.

Miia Koponen

I'm inclined to agree with Miia in that 'happy ever after' may not be realistic in our fast moving 21st century world. After all, everyone experiences challenges occasionally which would be impossible (and certainly unhealthy) to be happy about. However, I'd say being happy in a loving, supportive relationship sharing respect, intimacy, and closely identifying with a partner's values is absolutely possible and can happen for you.

This book explains so much more than understanding the basics of Interiors Therapy and creating your own Manifesto for Love™. We are going below the surface to dig out the deep-seated doubts and limiting beliefs holding you back in all areas of your life – not just romantic relationships but work, home, family, education and expectations.

It's going to support you to get clarity on how Interiors Therapy is useful even in the most minimal of homes:

❤ understand why the process is so much more powerful than simply de-cluttering and getting organised

- ❤ recognise the energetic impact of the possessions you keep

- ❤ clear clutter from your life at all levels

- ❤ identify and work towards the life and relationships you really want for yourself

- ❤ move ahead light, fresh and positive in the best place for you to enjoy your life no matter what

With expert guidance, your home, emotions, self-esteem and appearance will all support you to be your best self. So by the time you have completed your Interiors Therapy and you settle down to write your own Manifesto for Love™, you will know yourself better and be able to define the values and attributes of the person who will truly complement and be worthy of the real you.

Better still, you will be in a position to welcome them into your life.

PART I

Firm Foundations

To make the most of your investment in this book, the first stage is to understand where you are at right now, what has been holding you back and how your life will look when you achieve your ideal outcome.

Regardless of whether your plans are big or small, you'll want firm foundations to work from. That's what Part 1 is all about.

CHAPTER 2

What is your reality?

This is where I'm going to ask you to take a step back and look at yourself the way others perceive you... not your friends or your family, but a stranger, potentially the person you might spend the rest of your life with.

Come on, let's take a long hard stare in the mirror both metaphorically and physically. What do they see when they look at you, in fact, do they even notice you are there?

♥ Exercise 1

This is going to take you a while, but it really is worth grabbing a cuppa and working your way through it. It's going to explain a lot about how you feel, both about yourself and also your situation right now. And until you know where you are coming from, how can you know where you want to go?

Answer the following questions honestly – jot your answers down on a piece of paper, your phone, or just pencil them into the book – these are important factors in creating your Manifesto for Love™ so don't over-think or analyse your responses, just be honest and true to yourself.

For a more in-depth version of this exercise, visit the website at www.interiorstherapy.com/questions

- How old are you?

- Do you look your age?

- Are you physically fit, overweight, underweight, pretty much perfect?

- How are you emotionally?

- What's going on in your head?

- How did your last relationship make you feel while it was happening?

- What about afterwards?

- How is your self-esteem?

- Are you healthy, just right, a little unhealthy, really unhealthy?

- What is your best feature?

- Are you high maintenance, groomed, uninterested, average or careless with your appearance?

- Do you maintain good self-care or are you last on the list?

- Is your diet good, bad or indifferent?

- ❤ What are you passionate about?

- ❤ What hobbies do you have?

- ❤ What keeps you busy?

- ❤ Do you drink? How much?

- ❤ Do you smoke?

- ❤ Do you use recreational drugs?

- ❤ Are pets essential to your life?

- ❤ What gets you out of your home and gives you joy?

- ❤ Are you good at your job, do you care about your job, do you even have a job?

- ❤ Do you regularly complain, moan, share negative posts or memes?

- ❤ Are most of your words and actions positive or negative?

While we're at it, your perception of yourself is important too, so the next part of the exercise is to answer questions about your personal perspective to support the process. Again, don't think too hard about it and be honest with your responses. This is just for you.

- ❤ What is keeping you where you are?

- ❤ Do you feel good when you walk into your home at the end of the day?

- ❤ Where do you want to be in ten years, five years, next year, next month?

- ❤ Are you generally happy, sad, depressed, enthusiastic, just getting on?

- ❤ Do you see the best in every situation or expect the worst?

- ❤ How are your finances?

- ❤ What do you love to do on holiday?

- ❤ Is your home tidy, untidy, cluttered, minimalist, the lair of a hoarder, full of other people's stuff?

- ❤ How about the wardrobe? Do you wear everything in it? Do you even know what's in there?

- ❤ What is your idea of the perfect day? When did you last have one?

- ❤ When did you last have sex? Was it with someone you love?

- ❤ When was the last time you felt truly happy?

- ❤ When was the last time you laughed so much your tummy hurt?

- ❤ When did you last cry, and why?

- ❤ Do you feel appreciated?

- ❤ Do you feel grateful for what you have in your life?

- ❤ Do you value yourself?

- ❤ Do you feel valued by others?

- ❤ What would make you abundantly happy?

- ❤ What brings out the best in you?

- ❤ Are your parents' words and attitudes impacting on your life now?

- ❤ Who else dictates your thoughts?

Hold onto those answers, and if any other useful questions or ideas pop into your mind while you are working through these, note them and their answers too – this is all useful stuff!

By now you'll have quite a list describing who you are and how you feel about yourself. That's a great start because until you know where you are coming from and what is holding you back, you won't know where you want to go.

CHAPTER 3

Getting clear on what's holding you back

How do you really feel about your life? OK, that's a rhetorical question.

If you were already abundantly happy with everything in your life, you would not be here, working your way through this book, determined to create a new life with Interiors Therapy and ultimately implementing your Manifesto for Love™.

The vast majority of people who have yet to meet their ideal partner or who are not thriving in their current relationship are held back by three main challenges:

- The limiting beliefs we hold about ourselves

- The things and people we are surrounded by

- Our attitude to life

This chapter focuses on limiting beliefs and attitude to life. You've probably realised there is no 'quick fix' if things aren't going well in your life or relationship status. Instead, there will be multiple elements to identify and deal with. This part of the book is designed to get to grips with the internal stuff you've been holding onto and how your day to day attitude dictates the life you experience right now.

As you deep dive into the sticky beliefs, the revelations you experience will help you get a much clearer perspective on the impact of the things and people you surround yourself with. We will deal with those in Part 2 as you begin your Interiors Therapy adventure.

Limiting beliefs

Limiting beliefs are grown organically from our life experience, education, family behaviours and social conditioning. If throughout your life you have been hearing *"No one will ever love you," "You're rubbish," "All men are…", "You're stupid"* or the cracker I heard repeatedly from one less than charming companion, *"You are pathetic."* Then it's pretty tough to believe anything else.

So the point is, when you are hearing these things from people in authority, perhaps your parents, teachers or employers, maybe someone you love or have a strong emotional connection with like a partner or close friend, then those statements stick. If there is nothing in your understanding to challenge them, and you don't feel able to stand up to the individuals who are intent on demeaning you, their words grow deep roots into your psyche. They create limiting beliefs which become your reality.

It's fair to say we can't choose our family and all too easy for me to say, *"Hey, those thoughtless things they are saying? It's about them, not you."* It's precisely because they are our family that the statements hurt

us so much. Your parents and siblings know
press to make you feel good, and oh boy, the
lever to pull to rip the rug out from under you
shattered on the floor.

There are endless books which talk about far...   ...ps,
including how to manage them or at least cope during the time
you spend together. You don't need me to add my voice to those
specialists who are infinitely more experienced in family dynamics,
so I'll move on to the next group of people who you might have
allowed to have emotional power over you – your friends.

Do you remember when the opinions of school friends or foes were
so important to you that the things they said could make or break
your term? When being part of the popular group or invited to a
particular party meant you were accepted? Alternatively, perhaps
you were bullied by people who had once been trusted friends until
they turned their backs on you… it would have felt like the ultimate
betrayal.

The thing is, even though it could be many years since you were
at school, unless you left school very recently, you probably haven't
thought about it very much at all. Despite that, some of the mean,
nasty words are potentially still impacting on you now.

For anyone born before 1975, no matter what bullying you went
through at school, you can count yourself lucky to have been
born when you were. If you made a mistake, did something daft
or hooked up with the wrong person, memories were short and
incidents quickly forgotten. In extreme circumstances you could
move house, change your appearance and effectively rewrite your
history in your own words and start afresh… not anymore!

Now, whole lives are played out permanently on social media.
Comments, photos, video clips, tweets and connections across

of platforms ensure everything is remembered. There
vidence for each error of judgment, boozy night out and
inappropriate late-night post.

Aside from the opportunity we gift to cyber-bullies, every stupid thing we've ever done, said or shared on social media is waiting to bite back later – long after we've erased it from our own memories, it's available to new friends, potential lovers, employers, political parties and people who want to hurt or abuse. No one with a social media history is immune, no matter how tight the privacy settings.

As a side note, regardless of the situation or provocation, think carefully before you post negative comments about your own life. You are generating new limiting beliefs for yourself.

If you can't say anything nice, say nothing.

As a side note, remember that by posting gossip, speculation or abuse towards someone else, you become an online bully. Being a troll has no place in your new positive life and can do immense and lasting damage to others. Trust me, it will always backfire, and the person it will ultimately backfire on is you.

You don't have to tear down someone to feel good
about yourself, be kind.

Only you are responsible for how you treat others and for
what you put out in the world.

Laura Whitmore

My strong advice is to be kind in all your social media activities and only share comments you would be happy for someone to say about you. Celebrities, royals, politicians, those with different opinions, colour, sexuality, religion or background and yes, those people you simply don't like are all human. Just like you! If you don't appreciate what they are saying, it's simple, stop following them!

It is possible to disagree with someone's perspective without resorting to personal abuse or hate speak, and the faster you adopt this new layer of positivity in your life, the quicker you will see the benefits.

The next group of unhelpful commentators on your life will be those you met along the way at college, university or in your career. Careless, ill-considered statements from a tutor or boss can worm their way inside and become a factor in how we perceive ourselves.

Add in the impact of cruel comments from friends in adulthood, former lovers, people we look up to or even a stranger who says something derogatory, and we are awash with other people's beliefs which stick in our minds like manky old chewing gum.

When limiting beliefs remain unchallenged, they can become part of the way we define ourselves. We often adopt or accept them without stopping to consider whether there is genuine evidence for the belief at all. It's only when we actually take a step back, often with the help of a coach or therapist, and get to the root of where the belief came from, we realise it's complete rubbish.

If there are people in your life right now who choose to belittle you, say cruel things about your abilities, appearance, lifestyle or whatever, ask yourself how it is serving you to take their thoughts to heart.

Perhaps they believe they are being well-meaning. "I'm only saying this because I have your best interests at heart," is something one of my friends heard regularly from her mother. Those words almost always preceded a hurtful comment. My friend now politely asks her mother what evidence she has to justify her words and why she feels it necessary to be unpleasant. Gradually her mother is learning not to foist her own limiting beliefs on her only daughter.

Now, there are people who believe it's essential to say things which make you feel bad about yourself, often with the precursor, *"this is for your own good."* Contrast these inconsiderate characters with the people it always feels wonderful to be around. You know the ones I mean, those who make your heart sing when you spend time with them. Who point out the best in you, thrive in your company, just make you feel genuinely good when they walk into a room, or your phone lights up with a message from them. These are the people you can laugh with, talk to honestly, trust to encourage your dreams and whose shoulder you can dampen with your snot and tears and know they will still leave you feeling warm and safe.

Who do you trust more to give you feedback?

Your attitude to life

Think about the happiest people you know; friends, family members, colleagues, the bus driver who helps and has a kind word for every passenger… Do they complain about big things and small things? Criticise their friends or the people they love? Do they blame other people for their situation? No. They take responsibility, 'don't sweat the small stuff' and choose to be comfortable within themselves. When someone is happy and content, their happiness radiates positive energy which makes the people they connect with feel different.

But possibly thinking about them right now makes you feel all the more inadequate for having feelings of dissatisfaction, especially if you are emotionally able to take a step back and look at all of the wonderful things you already have in your life.

OK, let's get real here. YOU can CHOOSE who you want to be. Yes, you can! You can choose to have a positive outlook and see the best in situations and people, you can choose to be grateful for what you already have in your life, and you can start by understanding why the changes don't happen TO you, they have to happen IN you.

Each one of us is pure energy and energy responds to positive or negative stimulation.

If we focus on the negative elements of our lives, those things, situations or people whom we choose to complain about, criticise, resent, then we create more things to make us complain, criticise and resent.

Conversely, if we choose to find the positive, no matter what the circumstances, then we attract a happier outcome – it might be on a small scale, or it might be huge… it's always better than the negative option.

Take the person who invests time and thoughts in grizzling about their journey to work, the boss, home life, friends (if they have any), lack of money and life in general. Is life going to be a bundle of laughs or unbounded delight? No most definitely not! This is the sort of person who sucks every last morsel of joy from the people around them. Even if something wonderful happens, they will find the negative and moan about it to themselves and to anyone who will listen. They are exhausting to be around.

There are people who choose to live in exactly that negative place all the time. They are the Mr and Ms Angry of the world, moaning, hating, stirring, blaming, criticising, feeling victimised, but never taking responsibility for changing their outlook or attitude. Why should they? They have an unfailing belief that the reason they feel like that will be someone else's fault. Make sure you are not that person!

Conversely, consider the person who is relaxed about their journey to work, respects and appreciates colleagues and has a smile for everyone from the janitor to the CEO. They revel in a happy home life, many friends, might not have loads of money but are happy and enthusiastic about everything going on around them. If something sad or annoying happens, it might knock them briefly, but ultimately their positive attitude to life will bring them back on track.

Of course, these descriptions are extremes. We all have degrees of light and shade in our lives. Without occasional sadness, we wouldn't appreciate the good times. But if you think about the people who are surrounding you, with most you could pin a label on them – positive or negative? When the negative people outweigh the positive ones, that's when you need to carefully consider who you spend your time with.

There is a famous quote by motivational speaker Jim Rohn,

> *You are the average of the five people you spend most time with.*
>
> **Jim Rohn**

That's a good way to start reflecting on what is going on around you and ask yourself to consider whether the people closest to you are primarily positive or negative individuals. But as author and speaker David Burkus explains,

> *You're not the average of the FIVE people you surround yourself with. It's way bigger than that. You're the average of all the people who surround you. So take a look around and make sure you're in the right surroundings.*
>
> **David Burkus**

Now, I don't think Jim Rohn, David Burkus or anyone else is advocating you cutting off contact with your friends, relatives, colleagues, boss, or whatever without a second thought. That would be way too uncomfortable. No, what I've discovered over the last twenty years or so, is that as you start to work on becoming the person you want to be, the negative, flaky people fall away – perhaps they move house, change jobs, get a new boyfriend or just stop calling – and that's all as it should be.

And the interesting thing is that people from the past, who have been on their own journey and are now more on your new wavelength, often connect with you again.

I always think people come into your life for a purpose. They might be there for a minute, hour, day, month, decade, even a lifetime. Some come into our lives to teach us, others to show us what we are intrinsically capable of. Sometimes their role is to learn from us and often it is to challenge and question. Frankly, I'm also sure some are sent deliberately to irritate and see how far they can push us – but if you rise above their negativity, it's like jumping through a warm tropical waterfall into the next exciting phase of your life.

So taking all this into account, be prepared to part company with some of the people whose energy is holding you in a less than optimal place. Believe me; you will be better off without them long term – even if it initially feels like your world is collapsing in on you when they go.

So how are you going to start the process of changing the energy around you from low grade negativity to optimum positivity?

Step one is to feel good about it!

CHAPTER 4

Finding Gratitude

If you're in the habit of expecting the worst to happen, complaining, sharing negativity and being a victim, then the concept of finding things to be grateful for could be baffling... until you get it!

Suzanne Roynon

The more I read about the highly successful people I admire, (you know, the ones who have seemingly come from nowhere to enjoy the lifestyle, happiness, balanced relationship and inspirational plans for the future), the more it seems expressing gratitude is essential in their lives.

It's so good to be grateful, even for the smallest thing – the whole 'attitude of gratitude' thing has a very powerful impact on so many levels!

What is it like for you when someone says, "thank you", and you know they really mean it? Do you feel fabulous or just pay lip service to their words? Perhaps you even feel embarrassed and brush their gratitude to one side? Now consider the sensation when the situation is reversed, and your words or actions of thanks are pushed back at you? Leaves a slightly nasty taste, doesn't it?

I overheard a guy say to a lady he was chatting to at an event, *"Hey, you're looking amazing, your skin is glowing, and that dress really suits you."* Her response was this, *"How can you say that? I've put on 10kg and picked up this dress at a charity store because I'm too fat for my wardrobe."*

Have you ever thrown a compliment back into someone's face like that? The guy was so embarrassed he mumbled something and walked away. Later I found her in tears in the ladies' room. It turned out she had a massive crush on this guy, and it was the first time he'd really noticed her. She couldn't understand why he had walked away from their conversation.

The lady had no concept that throwing a compliment back at the giver not only exposed her limiting beliefs about her appearance, it also rejected his thoughts, words and actions, treating them, and therefore the man she adored, with contempt.

I'm saying whenever or wherever someone compliments you, accept those lovely words into your energy and know you are receiving a little piece of recognition for being here on the planet right here right now. Someone noticed you; someone took time to register your presence, and that person wanted you to know you are appreciated. Go with the flow! Welcome those words with a smile – whomever they come from.

For your part, say thank you for every service, kind gesture, action or reaction you experience. If you can't say it aloud to the person, or it relates to a situation or thing, say it inwardly with love. Speaking and meaning words of gratitude, even inwardly, carries a positive energetic charge which benefits you.

As I'm writing this section of the book, I'm conscious the plans I had for my weekend have all changed after a key meeting had to be postponed. I could be put out about this – after all, I had been looking forward to it. Instead, I am incredibly grateful for the new opportunities which have opened up as a result. I can lavish a little extra attention on my writing, go and meet a friend for supper and indulge in one of my favourite hobbies. None of this was possible until my plans were thrown up in the air.

The 'old' me would have been sulky and resentful and made it all about me. *"How dare they cancel the meeting at short notice, I planned my weekend around this. Why have I been treated this way?"* Today's society always seems to want to make us the victims in a situation and pin the blame on something or someone else.

Instead, I notice myself thinking, "OK, it isn't the right time to meet up, so I can do something else I love instead. I have no idea why it wasn't convenient to do the meeting today, and it doesn't matter at all. I know that for whatever reason, it wasn't the ideal time to get together, and when we catch up next week the time will be right for everyone involved."

Expressing Gratitude

There are so many ways you can fit expressing gratitude into your life. Do it at whichever time of day feels right for you. I prefer morning because it means every day starts well. Others choose the evening or just before bed as a way of counting their blessings and thinking positive thoughts just before sleep. What I'm trying to say is that it doesn't matter when or where you do it, just get grateful for what you already have in your life; for the people or things you want to draw into your life; for the little acts of kindness you experience through your day and for everything from the big things to the little tiny weeny ones.

For millennials or those whose smartphone is permanently welded to their hand, an app on the phone might be your best way forward. For others, a beautiful book. Some like to say the words out loud en route to work or run through them mentally in bed at the beginning or end of the day. I've seen gratitudes written on slips of paper and stored in a jar, Post-it notes, on whiteboards in offices and even written in washable ink on pebbles left on the beach.

A pioneering company talked of a way of incorporating gratitude into daily life by giving staff the option to declare three things they are grateful for as part of their computer login at the beginning of the day. The company knows this will focus the minds of the staff from the CEO to the interns in a positive place before they start work. This will promote wellbeing for staff and have a beneficial impact on morale and productivity. It's a win-win for everyone. Even if your company isn't this forward-thinking, you could choose to write your own three gratitudes as you turn on your PC each day.

There are thousands of ways you could express gratitude; choose one of these, research another alternative online, or make up one of your own – as Nike's advertising says, "Just do it."

The Gratitude Book

When I was inspired to start my first Gratitude Book, it didn't feel right to work from the front to the back of the book; I was interested in new beginnings rather than endings, so I started at the back and worked forward.

Turning over to the last double page, I wrote, "I am grateful" at the top of the right-hand page. Then,

1. *"I am grateful for this amazing new start in my life."*

It didn't take long to find ten things I was grateful for, and at the bottom of the page I wrote, "Thank you, Thank you, Thank you." Writing it three times over had a zingy effect and finished the page nicely.

After a day or two starting each morning in a positive frame of mind, I added in a new element to transform more negativity into positivity. On the left-hand page, I wrote the names of three people who were bothering me in some way – this might be because they were sick, sad, going through a tough time, or just plain irritating.

I knew worrying or being annoyed about them wouldn't help, but if I could send them love, I could knock out the negativity surrounding them in just a couple of words. So now the left-hand page was headed with 'Sending love to' and at least three names followed.

The final addition to the book beneath the daily names was to add the words 'Guidance for today'.

Sometimes a word or words just popped into my mind, other times I'd hear something on the radio which just 'felt' as though it fitted. The words were often random, but if I happened to look back on them, it turned out the word had been exactly what I needed to hear.

Every day starts well. My first thoughts are positive, spread love and give me wisdom.

As you get the hang of being grateful, you can extend your gratitude forward and enhance your day in other ways. For example, I've discovered I can be grateful before things have even happened,

"I am grateful for smooth journeys to and from London" means I expect and receive a relaxed and enjoyable train experience.

"I am grateful for meeting amazing new people today." It doesn't matter who I meet or where I see them; someone interesting will come into my life. I've met some lasting friends this way.

"I am grateful for the opportunities in my life."

"I am grateful for my healthy bank account."

"I am grateful for happy clients."

All of these statements are self-explanatory, and as the good energy surrounding your gratitude builds, it overflows into all areas of your life.

To paraphrase Napoleon Hill's seminal book, *Think and Grow Rich,*

What the mind can conceive and believe, it can achieve.

Napoleon Hill

Gratitude works for me, and it's a very simple way to start shifting your energy!

♥ Exercise 1

The sooner you start feeling gratitude, the faster you will feel different inside. Whether you do this in a book, on a scrap of paper or on your phone is up to you.

Begin your gratitude process by taking time now to write down ten things for which you are abundantly grateful. It doesn't matter when, where, who or how you experienced them, just find moments big or small and write them down.

If you want to make the exercise even more powerful, go for 20 or even 50 gratitudes.

You will feel your mood lighten as you do this.

♥ Exercise 2

Write a list of three or more people who are irritating, unwell, bereaved or you are concerned about, or situations which are really bugging you.

Now send each one love. Do this consciously and without preconditions or judgments. Even the tiniest shift in your thinking can make miracles happen.

Making a decision to love who you are

Lisa has been struggling recently. She is immensely talented, lives in a beautiful home and has a busy work and social life. Her partner Bobby was married previously and has grown-up children. They both have a lot to be grateful for, but Lisa's default setting has been, for quite some time, to feel cross and resentful.

Lisa had got into the habit of sharing negative, angry and political messaging online. When we got together, there would usually be something annoying her. She would talk unguardedly about members of the family, her partner, neighbours, people who had aggravated her in some way. Lisa believed she was always the victim of circumstances, and at Christmas, as often happens, there were some family rows which she blamed squarely on Bobby's kids. After days of arguments, it all came to a head, and Bobby said he wanted to leave.

Lisa was devastated and called to ask what she could do to put things right. I explained before anything else, Lisa had to fix her own negative thoughts, words, deeds, actions, beliefs, attitudes... and I wasn't just talking about the way his family had behaved, or what Bobby himself had done or not done. I meant every single part of her life and gave her some examples,

If you catch yourself swearing at another driver – stop!

If you see a negative post on social media, it's poisoning you – don't read it and certainly don't share it. Move on to something more positive.

If there are people constantly pumping negative words and images in your direction (on social media or anywhere else), they aren't your friends. They are toxic to your emotions and creating nasty vibes in and around you. Ditch them.

If you say mean things, even as a 'joke' they come back to hurt you from another, totally unrelated, direction.

If you complain about people and situations you can't control, it all flies back into your face – not necessarily immediately, but it's there in your energy waiting for an opportunity to backfire on you.

Does this sound familiar? If so, how is that working for you?

I explained to Lisa that the Law of Attraction is very clear, *what we state, we create'* and that we generate the situations we find ourselves in – either by thought, word or deed. So if I am in the situation where something I don't like happens, I look back at what I've been doing or saying which might have created it.

For example, I realised that simply by asking for an abundant lifestyle, I created abundant weight gain, – not at all what I had in mind! I need to reframe my words, be grateful for what I have learned and allow the excess weight to leave with my blessing.

And the interesting thing is this – when you purposefully and deliberately change your thinking, the situation around you changes. The negativity dissipates and often the things which no longer serve you, or have been feeding off your negative energy, starve and disappear.

When I made the decision on Boxing Day 2016 to change my vibe and send love into every negative situation, things started to change very quickly, and my destructive relationship was over by New Year. I'm not saying it was easy, straightforward or that I never think a negative thought... of course I do – but then I catch myself and remember it's going to bite back one way or another, so I reframe my thinking.

So taking the examples above:

Bad drivers: I repeat several times, "I am fortunate to be surrounded by competent drivers." (NB this is also good for clearing traffic jams!)

Negative posts or memes: Ignore or find a piece of good news for the day and share that instead.

Think NSC – never spread crap/complaints/ criticisms/cruelty.

Negative people on social media: Mute, or if you don't know them, Block them. Seriously, after a day or two, you won't miss them.

When you are tempted to say something negative about a person or situation, whether it's a family member or the impolite barista, send them love instead – even if you have to do it through gritted teeth at first.

If you genuinely have something to complain about, instead of complaining to anyone who will listen (that just spreads negativity), send a brief, polite email or telephone the person who *can* do something about it. Send the situation good vibes, maybe offer a proactive solution rather than just grumbling. You'll be amazed just how much more effective you can be – and feel good about it too.

Then actively do anything you can to spread kindness – I'm a big fan of Random Acts of Kindness, and they don't have to cost anything at all. There are loads of lists of ideas on the internet for things you can do which might just change someone's life for the better. And if you are open to doing Random Acts of Kindness, then more opportunities to do them come along.

It's fair to say the emotional climate in the UK has been impacting people in so many negative ways. It has been deliberately ramped up by sharing disinformation designed to inflame and stoke anger, distrust, fear and dissatisfaction. That same energy impacts on homes, relationships, colleagues and the people we love. By feeding off it and reading/sharing/talking about negative stuff, we invite it into our homes, encourage it, fatten it up and then wonder why our lives fall apart.

I don't think it's a coincidence that the happiest people I know seldom watch TV news and actively change the subject when people are being negative around them. They consciously spread good, positive messages. They are happy as their default setting. Good things happen, and lovely opportunities come to them.

But if they sink or let worry overtake them… WALLOP! It backfires, and something happens which causes pain, inconvenience, loss. It's a hard lesson to learn – and as no one is perfect, we have to keep learning it over and over again.

The fact is, there is little we can do personally about the dishonest politicians except vote them out when the opportunity arises. However, we can be a part of slowing the flow of hatred by actively:

a. being positive in words and actions

b. seeing both perspectives and having a balanced view

c. above all be kind and think kind thoughts about anyone and everyone you come into contact with or who is impacting on your life in some way.

Lisa had been feeling hurt and under attack. Her emotional pain attracted more reasons to be upset which she shared widely. Like a cyclone, she spun with anger and snide comments, hateful messages, complaints and criticism of Bobby, his kids and the world in general and WHAM! Her life came crashing down around her.

The only person who could stop this was Lisa.

Lisa came to understand Bobby felt vulnerable, and when she exuded bad vibes, he sunk further, and the negativity built up around him. Bobby couldn't see his kids' behaviour as unacceptable because he was surrounded by so much of Lisa's negativity; it seemed perfectly reasonable. Nothing could change until the atmosphere around Bobby changed – and that had to start with Lisa.

If you are in a similar situation, it has to start with you too – no matter how much my saying that stings!

And right now, you are sitting pretty. It might not feel like it, but you are. Big time.

You can choose to lead your life and experience back into a more positive place and let the energy shift around you.

Now I'm not saying this will fix everything overnight – and ultimately, some relationships which are not serving you will not survive. Regardless of how painful that situation is, it will be for the best long term.

Alternatively, when the bleak energy dissipates, you'll each remember why you fell in love in the first place.

I've seen it happen both ways, and in each situation, it worked out for the best. But the foundation has to be energy changes from negative to positive, and the only person who can start this is you.

CHAPTER 5

The foundation of Interiors Therapy

My interest in Feng Shui began in the last year of my marriage, when, struggling with a wretched combination of postnatal depression and knowing divorce was looming, I longed to make sense of my life.

The house felt like a prison, there was no money to spend, interest rates were high, the house was in negative equity, and I had no job. We were living in a four-bedroom place on a quiet road in a small market town. It had been my 'roses round the door' dream home and my first big Law of Attraction manifesting success (not that I knew anything about the Law of Attraction back then). Inside the house, we were surrounded by all the things we had bought while we were happy – cute cottagey stuff, dried flowers, copper kettles, prints and pictures on the wall, collections of CDs, photos, books, all the wedding presents. It was very twee, horribly cluttered and absolutely stifling.

I read the three books on Feng Shui available at the time and followed the instructions carefully. But nothing changed; in fact, everything just got worse. Now I look back, none of those books mentioned anything about dealing with clutter. I still had that lesson to learn.

When I made the decision to leave my marriage with my baby daughter, I took our clothes, some books and a few toys. It was a decision based on the practicality of briefly moving back into my childhood bedroom in my parents' home. There wasn't room for anything else. From there we got a place in a hostel for the homeless and finally a local authority flat. When we moved to the hostel, I asked my ex for a single bed, sofa bed, some curtains and a box of photos. And that was it. After nine years together and collecting a houseful of stuff, none of it counted for anything in my life.

But hey, collecting clutter wasn't done with me yet. Not by a long way!

Because no sooner had I moved into the flat; I started looking for things to fill it with. This time it was plants, crystals, yet more books, cushions and loads of fairies, which I convinced myself were for my daughter's benefit.

By this time I was working in a long-term temp job, so there was a little money to spend. My daughter spent each weekend with her dad which meant I could get out and meet new people and expand my knowledge.

My new romance foundered because I was not a catholic, which evidently made me an unsuitable life partner in the eyes of his mother, although the man himself never set foot in a church! Soon afterwards, I was assaulted by an unstable individual who became a stalker. It was time to look at my life and understand the patterns I had created.

The men who had been significant to me all had dominant mothers. Their idea of a good time involved a lot of alcohol (the men, not the mothers), and we had no real interests in common aside from fancying one another. It wasn't really a great basis for any relationship, but I'd been too fixated on being with 'someone' to notice.

I holed up in the flat and spent a lot of time on self-development, attending Mind Body Spirit events and investing in my spirituality. The whole religious prejudice thing had really hurt, and I wanted to understand why organised religion constricts the concept of God being about 'Love'. I started to detach from established religion and see 'God' more as an omnipresent universal power or energy.

The stalker was playing havoc with my mental health. He would hang about outside the flat staring up at the window. Every now and then he would be arrested and kept on remand, giving a brief respite, but he would be back again within a few weeks. It was no way to live.

That's when a particularly wonderful book called *Creating Sacred Space with Feng Shui* came into my life. It was written by Karen Kingston who, as it happened, was doing a workshop at the Mind Body and Spirit Festival in London later that year. I read and re-read the book before I went to the workshop. There was a chapter about clearing clutter, and I found myself reviewing every part of the flat to see where I was hiding stuff which might be holding me back... And there was loads – again!

Why was I keeping gardening books when I had no garden? What was the point of having hundreds of photos of my ex-husband's family? Why did I still have love letters from teenage boyfriends, and how was it serving me to hold on to the court documents from the assault case?

As I dumped, ditched and donated my possessions, I started to feel better, more focused and lighter. There was no doubt about it; I felt and looked fabulous.

I got an opportunity to be featured in the *Daily Mail* in one of their makeover articles, and as a result received two life coaching sessions with 'Queen of Coaches' Fiona Harrold, at a time long before Life Coaching became a thing. Fiona helped shift my perspective on where I was going.

My temp job turned into a full-time position, and the salary increased significantly. The stalker went to prison for attacking someone else. The whole clutter-clearing thing was really working for me.

I went along to Karen Kingston's workshop and met the lady herself. I sat on the front row, feeling that I was in completely the right place and knowing this was the beginning of a journey, there was much more to learn. I really had just scratched the surface.

I saved frantically and asked Karen Kingston to spaceclear my flat personally. She brought a trainee with her, and I watched spellbound as they worked what really felt like magic, lifting the energy to the point where it felt as though everything glowed. The Feng Shui ideas and suggestions were swiftly followed.

Karen Kingston asked me to be precise about what I wanted in my life. That was simple: a happy child, a home where I felt safe, to be in a relationship with someone who loved me and have enough money to enjoy myself... so happiness, love and security, pretty much the same as everyone else in the world!

In the months that followed, I got another pay rise and promotion, making me one of the youngest managers in the organisation, I met a really lovely man, and the Universe set the wheels in motion for me to move into a pretty little house overlooking fields and trees.

It took three years for me to go from homeless to home-owner – a huge achievement.

So that was my introduction to the power of clearing clutter and starting afresh.

Did I learn my lesson? No, of course not! Now you know why this book has taken 17 years to write!

I moved into the house and started acquiring stuff – again!

Books, DVDs, albums of photos, computer stuff, kitchenware, statues, candles, more twee things (I was in the country after all!), ornaments, vases, pictures, mirrors, the stuff just kept on coming right through the door. My Feng Shui books just joined the clutter in the new built-in cupboards I'd bought to store it all.

The job started to get challenging; the lovely man moved on, money got tight, unsatisfactory boyfriends came and went. A couple of years staggered by and I found myself at a Mind Body Spirit event in Bedford, where I met two remarkable ladies. The first was Feng Shui expert Vanessa Edwards – you'll meet her properly later. The second was Alison Knox of Everyday Angels art, an amazing artist whose work inspires and delights me.

I went home that afternoon, floating on a cloud of good vibes. I looked at all the stuff stagnating in my space. Crammed bookshelves were dusty, there was no room in the cupboards, and the energy in the house was thick with dissatisfaction.

I was so cross with myself for allowing the clutter to creep up on me again. I was about to be 40, and before life could begin, the clutter had to go.

It was quicker this time. The clutter flew out of the door as I pulled an 'all-nighter' to get it done before my daughter came home the next day. Vanessa Edwards visited a few weeks later, and we space cleared the residual unhappy energy, checked the Feng Shui placement and disposed of some unhelpful images. For the first time, I began to understand the implications of imagery.

Vanessa Edwards encouraged me to engage more with female friends and suggested I might enjoy partner dancing as a healthy way of receiving human contact… As singletons will know, being held for more than a moment or two is one of the things you miss the most when you don't have a significant other in your life. I put 'try Ceroc' (a form of modern jive dancing) on my list of things to do.

The other thing I was inspired to do as my birthday approached was make a list of the things which were important to me in a relationship… I called it my 'Manifesto'.

A month later, 60 guests came to my 40th birthday party. Among them, new friends and others who had been with me for years. We had a mini festival, dancing and singing in the garden. The house felt happy again.

Soon afterwards, I started dancing Ceroc, which you can do at venues all over the country. Three weeks after that, a stranger walked across an empty dance floor to ask me to dance. On his first visit to my home, he said how lovely it felt and how he could really imagine living there with me. He scored highly on everything I had included on my Manifesto. We were together for 11 years.

PART II

Interiors Therapy

Oh! Will you never let me be?
Oh! Will you never set me free?
The ties that bound us
Are still around us
There's no escape that I can see

And still those little things remain
That bring me happiness or pain
A cigarette that bears a lipstick's traces
An airline ticket to romantic places

And still my heart has wings
These foolish things remind me of you

These Foolish Things
Holt Marvell & Jack Strachey

Interiors Therapy is so much more than de-cluttering or organising. It's a dynamic combination of life coaching, clearing, reclaiming and redefining thought and space with a sprinkling of Feng Shui.

The method gained global recognition when Jennifer Aniston used an Interiors Therapist to cleanse emotional and physical baggage from her LA mansion following the end of her marriage to Justin Theroux.

While Interiors Therapy is relatively new to the UK, its popularity soared as people recognised the myriad ways homes and personal effects impact on emotions, health, success and the ability to move on from life's inevitable challenges.

Holding onto possessions after a relationship breakdown or death of a loved one is a high-speed route to emotional blockages.

Suzanne Roynon

Clients describe stress, family and relationship problems, guilt, weight gain, anxiety or depression and blame themselves. They repeat the same patterns and mistakes time and again with different people and don't realise their belongings are the trigger.

Interiors Therapy is non-judgmental. By breaking the cycle of fear and loss, you regain control of your surroundings and freedom to live life as you choose, perhaps for the first time.

Frequently clients want to work with me because they feel 'something is missing' from their life. Even with a dazzlingly successful career, it's easy to experience voids elsewhere.

One lonely high-flying international banker found new love within a month of his Interiors Therapy. Other clients report outcomes such as boosted self-esteem, promotions, swift house sales, opportunities, travel, windfalls, love and contentment, and feeling unblocked after years of stagnation.

Interiors Therapy works for every home regardless of size, contents and location. From studio apartments to family homes and the estates of nobility, Interiors Therapy focuses on empowering you to take control, release years of negativity and thrive in a lighter, more positive lifestyle. If you are happy in your home and feel gratitude for the things you love, then every day starts well, and who can argue with that?

CHAPTER 6

Clarity about your possessions

Over the past twenty years or so as I've studied, researched, trained, experimented and practised the various elements of the what I now refer to as 'Interiors Therapy,' I've realised there are five key areas to the process.

With the first, once you master this, everything that's been going on in your life just starts to make more sense, but if you don't get it, or you stubbornly put your fingers in your ears and say 'la la la' rather than consider the potential damage your possessions can create, things are just going to stay the same... You need clarity.

Maybe until now you haven't associated the challenges at work, in your relationships, even with your health and stress levels with the things you keep around you. Perhaps you are so used to feeling this way it's become your normal – and you've almost given up expecting anything better.

Gaining clarity about the impact of things you keep around you is the first stage to understanding why you're experiencing obstacles and disappointments right now.

Eighteen years after we first worked together, I re-connected with 'Queen of Coaches' Fiona Harrold for some phenomenal mentoring. Fiona invited me to meet her at the home of a friend, conveniently located in central London. As Fiona made tea, I looked around the sitting room of the smart mansion block apartment.

"This friend of yours Fiona, is she in a controlling relationship, or does she feel she's trapped in a cage somehow?"

Fiona nearly dropped the tea tray and confirmed that yes indeed, to her relief the friend had just escaped one very controlling man and was now dating again – although she was concerned the new relationship was following a similar pattern.

I explained the fruit bowl in the shape of a cage situated in front of a very elegant mirror in the Feng Shui 'relationship area' of the room was creating or at least exacerbating these feelings of being controlled or in a cage.

There were other clear pointers to describe the challenging situation for Fiona's friend at that time, and Fiona was keen to help her move forward.

Later, after the friend disposed of the fruit bowl, she lost interest in the new controlling man and met someone infinitely kinder.

My clients are often astonished by what their home says about them, and it's important to say each home is as unique as the person or people who live there.

Clarity shows you how your possessions reflect and amplify what's going on in your life, and when you get there, it's a light bulb moment. Once you get this, you'll be part of the small percentage of people who understand why their personal environment impacts so dramatically on their day to day life.

But I have to tell you; it isn't straightforward. Yes, of course, there will be certain red flags which work for every home, (cages being one of them), but because you are an individual, your Interiors Therapy will be too.

The method I use and teach is the Forensic Focus Formula. It looks in-depth at the situation you are in at work, with your health, wealth and relationships and opens your eyes to the ways in which your possessions are causing or amplifying it for you.

Even people with the most minimal homes can inadvertently store negative stagnant energy in just a few possessions. Imagine how energy is magnified in a busy, crowded home or one filled with possessions handed down from one generation to the next.

Using the formula, you can compare the areas in which you are successful with those where you desire change for the better.

When I have the pleasure of working one to one with clients, I can often look around their homes without knowing anything about them and provide them with an accurate summary of their current significant concerns or issues.

If they have already given me some background, it's even easier to identify the trigger possessions. These are often art, furniture, images, even ornaments, but what often surprises people the most is that the simplest, most insignificant things can have the biggest impact.

Much as I'd love this book to identify every potential trigger for you, that's simply not practical, after all, you and your situation are unique, and that's what makes you so special.

Instead, I will highlight key elements and possessions to look out for across the specific areas of your home and see what revelations you experience.

However, before we get to the big triggers, I need to explain a little more about the 'areas' I've been going on about.

CHAPTER 7

Very basic Western Feng Shui

Firstly, I want to give you a little grounding in Feng Shui. Whether you subscribe to the concept, already know a little about it, want to know more, or you regard it as hogwash, this section will give you a clearer understanding of various references and phrases in the following pages and provide a more informed view of the position of various items in your home.

Feng Shui, the oriental art of placement, has been used in China and the Far East for over 5000 years. Originally it was implemented by agricultural societies to identify the perfect position for a home. Over the centuries it has been refined, disseminated and adapted to reflect modern life, high rise homes and businesses around the world.

Feng Shui advocates there are nine key areas of life known as 'guas' and the ideal design of the home should incorporate space for each one.

The guas or areas of life are defined as follows:

- Wealth, Blessings, Abundance

- Fame, Recognition

- Relationships

- Family and Ancestors

- Health and Wellbeing

- Children, Projects and New Beginnings

- Knowledge and Spirituality

- Career and Life Path

- Travel and Helpful friends

There are two main methods or 'schools' of Feng Shui. The original or traditional 'Classic' or 'Chinese' Feng Shui uses compass directions to identify and classify the position of the areas or 'guas' of your home and uses an octagonal design for its area map or 'bagua' to identify them. It incorporates I Ching symbols along with geographic and elemental information and you can see a diagram on the next page.

The Traditional, Classic or Chinese Feng Shui Bagua looks like this:

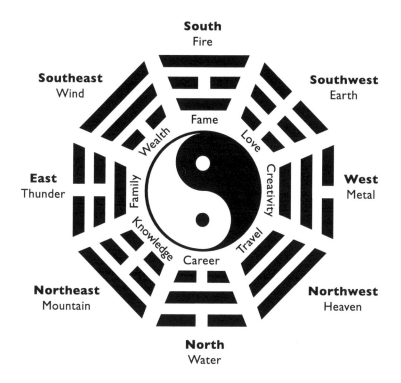

The Western version of Feng Shui, sometimes known as Black Hat, 'Three Gate' or 'Main Door' Feng Shui uses the main entrance of the home as the foundation or baseline of the Feng Shui map or 'Bagua'.

The theory is that the main door is where the 'Chi' or life force energy enters the home.

The Western Feng Shui Bagua looks like this:

Wealth and Blessings	Fame and Recognition	Relationships and Love
Family and Ancestors	Health and Wellbeing	Children/ Projects/ New Beginnings
Knowledge and Spirituality	Career and Life Path	Travel and Helpful Friends

↖ ↑ ↗

Doorway

The main entrance to the home, or if you are using this at individual room level, the doorway you use most to enter the room is placed on the bottom line of the grid. It can sit anywhere along the bottom line. Depending on where the main door is situated in your home it could be in the area or gua for Knowledge and Spirituality, Career and Life Path or Travel and Helpful friends – or even overlap two of the areas.

♥ Exercise

Draw a basic floor plan of your home and overlay the bagua onto it. If you have a printed floor plan, perhaps from an estate agent or architect, this makes your bagua even more accurate.

If you share part of a larger building, an apartment or annexe, or you are living in shared accommodation, your floor plan should purely reflect the part of the building that is your space. Draw it from your main door as if there were nothing else around it.

If you are lucky enough to have a square or rectangular house, that's fantastic, and the house will be balanced with all your areas or guas present.

In fact, if you are planning to move house anytime soon, this is something well worth considering for the ideal property.

These are the basic shapes of houses with all bagua areas present:

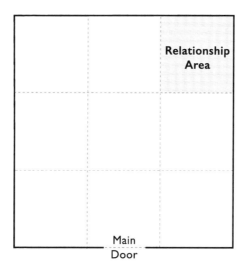

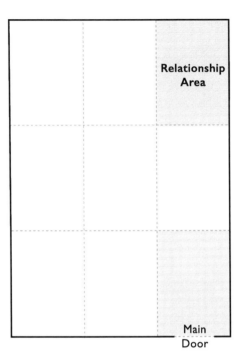

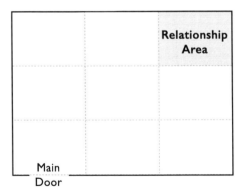

If your floor plan is a peculiar shape – perhaps you have an extension or a side return, or you live in an apartment with cut out communal areas for stairs and lobbies – then you are missing part or all of one or more guas. Don't panic, there are cures and remedies to deal with this, but you might find it explains quite a bit about your current situation.

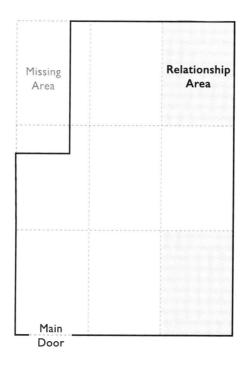

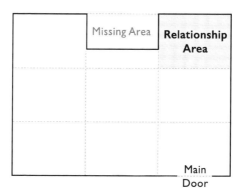

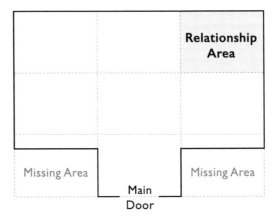

Although it's not the whole story, Feng Shui is an important element of Interiors Therapy. There are hundreds of books on the subject of both Traditional and Western Feng Shui which cover the principles in much greater depth than is possible here. If you'd like to know more, a few of the authors I have found particularly helpful are listed at the back of this book.

CHAPTER 8

Big triggers and aha moments

There are a variety of trigger points to look out for in Interiors Therapy, and this is where the process takes a significant step away from basic de-cluttering and organising.

An Interiors Therapist might also be a de-cluttering expert, but a Professional De-clutterer may not have the knowledge of energy work, Feng Shui, life coaching, space clearing and other elements which are incorporated into the Interiors Therapy process.

You see, in Interiors Therapy, identifying clutter and getting organised is just a small part of the process. We're not simply getting rid of things you no longer use and putting the rest in neat storage. Instead, I'm asking you to look at everything you own. Yes, it might traditionally be regarded as clutter, but it can just as easily be in active use and still be unsupportive of the life, relationship and experiences you desire to have in your life going forward.

So for the time being, we're not looking for clutter (I'm guessing you already have a fair idea where you keep that anyway!), we're actually getting clarity about the impact of the other possessions you keep around you. For ease, I've defined them in the following categories:

- Art, including photos, sculpture, imagery
- Furniture
- Single items
- Décor
- Damaged or broken items
- Lighting
- Plants
- Use of rooms
- Cupboards and storage
- Generational or second hand/repurposed/vintage items
- The energy

This section could become a whole book in its own right, so I'm restraining myself from creating the equivalent of *War and Peace*.

Instead, I'll give you an overview of what to look out for in your own home and illustrate it with a story or stories from my practice.

There are three main strands to this clarity element of Interiors Therapy, and you have to be honest with yourself right from the start.

❤ Perception – What is the item saying or depicting?

❤ Emotion – How does it make you feel?

❤ Reflection – What memories are associated with it?

What is the item saying or depicting?

This is where you may have to detach from your feelings about the item and look at it from a different perspective. That's not always easy, and sometimes you might need to move the item to a different position than you are used to seeing it in to really assess it carefully.

For example, you might see a poster of Darth Vader which reminds you at face value of your favourite movie. I see a masked, lonely, ostracised man. When I spot him in a home, he tells me a lot about the single, (usually) male occupant who struggles to make lasting real-life friendships and longs to be loved.

Even when I find good old Darth in the home of a couple or family, asking a few questions generally reveals the man or one of the children is hard to reach, emotionally distant and unwilling to engage.

That's just one example, there are many more, but hopefully, it's got you thinking.

How does it make you feel?

It is really important to be aware of the feeling, sensation, thoughts or words which come to mind when you look at an object or pick it up.

If the automatic response is a tightening of the chest, a feeling of fear, sadness, deep loss, anger or anything along those lines, then the item is a prime candidate for removal.

If instead it fills you with delight, overwhelms you with happiness and makes you smile, then that's fantastic. That's how you should feel about everything you own or keep around you.

As an example, finding a long lost ring can trigger either delight or pain. I've worked with people who have unearthed the wedding ring from a past unhappy marriage while working on their Interiors Therapy. When they realise they are still hosting the energy of a difficult relationship hidden away in a dark corner, it can be deeply upsetting.

But in the same vein for a happily married person or widow who has lost the love of her life, finding a treasured ring, perhaps an engagement or eternity ring misplaced at some time in the past can evoke beautiful tears of joy.

It all depends on individual circumstances, and that's why Interiors Therapy is such a complex and interesting process.

What memories are associated with it?

Now this can be a minefield, so bear with me.

Firstly, anything which (as above) generates memories of fear, anger, sadness, pain, anguish, and trauma should not be given houseroom.

Take Hailey's chest of drawers. It was a perfectly serviceable, actually rather lovely piece of furniture, solid oak and expensive. It was one of the few items Hailey kept from the marital home after the end of her marriage. The chest of drawers sat in Hailey's bedroom and was full of her clothes.

Logically there was no reason to question the presence of the chest of drawers in Hailey's life.

However, when Hailey explained she didn't like to sleep in that room and preferred to sleep on a single bed in the room next door, it was clear something was unsettling the energy in the main bedroom.

My first question is always about the bed – but Hailey had invested in a new, very comfortable bed which she absolutely loved, so it wasn't that.

Next we reviewed the contents of the drawers and the wardrobe. The energy shifted slightly, but Hailey was still visibly edgy.

As we started to fold Hailey's clothes ready to put them away in the drawers, she recalled various unhappy incidents from her marriage which had taken place in the bedroom of her old home. I asked her to describe what she was seeing, and Hailey visualised her ex-husband leaning against the chest of drawers bellowing at her while she cowered in fear.

As soon as she made the connection, Hailey recognised why the subconscious memories associated with the chest of drawers made it impossible for her to relax in her bedroom. The drawers were removed from the house altogether, and Hailey now loves the revitalising energy in her bedroom.

That's a very simplistic overview, and I'm going to immediately acknowledge that sometimes, for a range of reasons, things which trigger unhappy feelings or memories have to be kept.

Keeping things you really don't want because you have to…

This might include legal papers connected to a divorce or court case. Property which belongs to someone else or things you feel obliged to keep for your own reasons (we'll get to those later).

If you do have to hold onto items which engender negativity for you, take a look at the Feng Shui bagua for your home and put them in the 'least worst place'. In the majority of homes, this might be the Family and Ancestors area which represents your history and past. Wherever you decide to keep them, as soon as you are able to dispose of or pass them on, let them go.

OK, so we've covered the basics of perception, emotion and reflection which are essential to begin your process of un-sticking your life and current situation.

Everything you own or keep around you is going to present you with either a good trigger, a bad trigger or have no trigger, which for the sake of clarity, we're going to call a neutral trigger.

If you are currently experiencing any form of depression or are taking mood-altering medication, you might feel everything has a neutral trigger simply because your emotions have been flattened by the drugs or as a self-preservation response by your mind. In this situation, please focus on the perception and reflection actions to help make your decisions.

For each item in the various categories, you are going to implement the perception, emotion and reflection tools you've already learned.

Look closely at the item, see it with fresh eyes, or pick it up if you need to and detach yourself from the habit of having it in your space.

The first couple of times you do this, say with a picture or photo, it might take a little while to reach a conclusion about whether the item enhances your life or is actually creating a little pool of negativity at a conscious or subconscious level.

But believe me, you can get good at it very quickly if you are really ready to make a transformational change.

It's wise to bear in mind that sometimes an item you love is simply in the wrong place. By moving it to a more appropriate location, you resolve any potential problem it is creating. However, if you've accepted the item really isn't serving you, then you'll feel much more comfortable about letting it go.

If you're completely stuck with making a judgment on something, get an unbiased opinion from a friend you trust (make sure they didn't give it to you in the first place!). Sometimes we become so blind to possessions we don't notice them at all.

So as you begin the process, bear in mind that sometimes you'll have an immediate gut instinct when it comes to an item. Trust it. There will be a good reason for that reaction. If you know deep down something is unhelpful to you, but you are too stubborn to accept the obvious, think back to other times in your life when you have been entrenched in a particular position – how did that work out for you?

Most of the time, by taking a detached view, you'll know very quickly which of your possessions are beneficial and which are holding you back.

You aren't getting rid of anything right now; you are just assessing what you have and how it feels.

Let's get started by reviewing the questions you could ask yourself and then follow the prompts over the following pages to review your possessions and how they are working for you.

Here are the questions, see how you go…

Perception actions:

1. Detach yourself from the origin of the piece and who gave it to you.

2. What is it saying to you?

3. What does owning it say about you?

4. If you saw it in someone else's house, what would you think?

5. How would someone seeing it for the first time describe it?

6. Why do you keep it?

7. How is it serving you?

Emotion actions:

1. How does it make you feel?

2. If it wasn't there anymore, would it matter?

3. Is it a good trigger?

4. Is it a bad trigger?

5. Is it a neutral trigger?

Reflection actions:

1. Which Feng Shui 'gua' or area is it situated in?

2. Does the item feel auspicious for the Feng Shui area?

3. Where did it come from?

4. Did you acquire it legitimately?

5. Do you still like the person who gave it to you?

6. Did you buy it for the right reasons?

7. Are you keeping it for a negative reason? (Including to prevent someone else having it, vengeance, spite or selfishness.)

8. Is it still appropriate for your life now?

9. Are you keeping it out of habit or obligation?

10. What purpose does it have?

11. If you were moving to the home of your dreams, would you still display it there?

❤ Art, including photos, imagery, sculpture

I want you to go around your entire home and look at everything on the wall, on display in cabinets, on shelves, the things stuck to the fridge, left on the mantelpiece or stacked up in the corner – all the photos, ornaments, kitsch gifts, sculpture, art, paintings, cards. We're looking for anything remotely decorative.

I used the example of Darth Vader earlier in this section because his dark, gloomy countenance crops up so frequently in the homes of lonely, unhappy or dissatisfied people.

Another 'regular' is Frida Kahlo, who rocks up in the homes where the occupants, mostly women, have or are experiencing anxiety or depression.

Both these subjects also fit into a later category about single images, so I'm going to move on to the less obvious elements to look out for.

Images of anyone undernourished, desperate, poor, afraid, under attack, fighting, sad, lonely, abandoned, lost, neglected, abused, aggressive or any other negative content are going to be bad news for both your Feng Shui and your subconscious emotional state.

Anything relating to ex-partners, where the relationship ended with one or both parties getting hurt will have a residual impact on your relationship energy. Even if it's a gift or a beautiful photograph of you or a place you visited together, if you know your ex was behind the camera or with you there, it's time to ask yourself why you keep it.

Abstracts. These paintings can engender anger, confusion or both. Think very carefully before you buy them and never keep them in the areas relating to wealth, health, relationships or new beginnings.

Anything made of dried flowers. These flowers are dead energy, and that's symbology you don't need in your home. Please don't be like the lady who mounted two twig and dried flower hearts above the sofa she shared with her partner and then wondered why the relationship was dead two months later.

People who cover their fridges with magnets are always surprised when I ask if they struggle with their weight. Magnets are frequently made in bright colours designed to attract attention. They lure us to wherever we place them – and if that's the fridge, the obvious next action is to open the door and tuck in.

If you really love random gifts, vases, kitsch and ironic items, great. If you are keeping them to make a point or because you feel obliged to, you don't!

♥   Furniture

As with Hailey and her chest of drawers, it may well be you have items of furniture which trigger unhappy or unhealthy memories.

Furniture is often used as a weapon in a fraught divorce. This does no one any good, and the energy of the furniture is often tainted. One lady was thrilled to have won the battle to keep her luxurious three-piece suite after her relationship ended, only to find she preferred sitting at the dining room table with her friends and never used the sofas she had curled up on with her partner.

Ultimately, she gave the furniture away, bought an inexpensive replacement set and is now infinitely happier.

Bryan asked me to work with him because he was struggling to move on from his old relationship. He was still angry at his ex-wife's decision to end their marriage three years earlier. He acknowledged that he hadn't been faithful and had lost interest in his wife long before the marriage ended, but he resented that she walked out. He felt he was a victim and wanted to hurt her.

Bryan had held onto an antique nursing chair his ex-wife inherited from her grandmother. He had no need for it, but knew his ex-wife and her new partner were expecting a baby so, despite her reasonable request to have the chair, he kept it out of spite.

You can probably imagine that Bryan's energy wasn't remotely conducive to meeting and forming a relationship with someone new.

Ultimately, after several sessions of Interiors Therapy and coaching to reframe his thinking, Bryan made the decision to return the chair and sent it to his ex-wife with flowers and a heartfelt, deeply apologetic letter.

After the triggers for Bryan's anger disappeared, he began to feel better. He got a new job with higher pay, moved to a different town and is now dating again.

❤ Single items

We touched on this earlier, but I really can't emphasise enough how single energy attaches itself to single things.

It's interesting that for decorative items – lamps, pictures, cushions, candles etc. a united couple will often buy one each, whereas a singleton will only buy one.

In Feng Shui, pair, duo or couple energy is incredibly powerful and it is always recommended that if you want to be in a relationship or to have companionship around you, you have matching lamps, two chairs at the table, two hearts and that you avoid single images in any form – even cute kittens, dogs, puppies or baby elephants.

Have a good look around your home? If you are single, are you also surrounded by single items? One lady counted 71 single images in her home.

Michael, a middle-aged man living in rented accommodation since his divorce some years earlier was keen to meet someone new – at least that's what he told me during our initial Skype consultation from his home in Ohio.

But his home was replete with paintings and photographs of lone wolves, individual Indian Chiefs and the obligatory Darth Vader. He had a dining table with one seat, and a large La-z-boy chair in front of the TV. His bedroom had only one bedside table and a single lamp. It wasn't that he couldn't afford anything more – on the contrary, Michael had executive status and plenty of money to spare.

There was nothing remotely indicative of Michael's desire for love or even company. Instead, he had thrown himself into a monk-like solitude.

Bit by bit, Michael reviewed his possessions, explaining what they meant to him when he bought them and how they made him feel now. Gradually he added pair energy to his home and found his smile again. He joined a few mixed sport clubs and enjoys a busy social life. He's realised while he likes his own space he prefers being with a group of people. He turned from lone wolf to being part of a pack, and for now, it suits him very nicely.

❤ Décor

Every part of your home reflects your Feng Shui, so if you have stains, rips, scuffs, knocks and bumps around your home, they are often reflected in the gua for that area of your life.

Have a torn carpet in your Family and Ancestors area? Are your family breaking apart or being unsupportive?

Have a stain in the Fame and Recognition area? Perhaps your reputation is being damaged or are you being passed over for promotion?

Scuffs in your career area? Clean them up and give your career the refresh it deserves.

Leaks, mould and damp are a particular concern. A leak symbolises money draining away from your home regardless of which gua it sits in. Dripping taps, perennially running cisterns, damaged sealant around a shower causing nasty smells, poorly fitting connections to white goods all reflect financial challenges. Get them fixed without delay.

❤ Damaged or broken items

If something electrical you need, use or love is broken, fix it. If it can't be fixed, get rid of it. Never leave it on a shelf or in a cupboard exuding damaged energy into that gua.

I often see chipped or cracked ornaments in the homes of people whose lives aren't going as they would like them to. Yes, it sometimes feels brutal to dump the little china fish your Mother gave you, but it's stuck together with glue, missing a fin and looking very sorry for itself – just like you!

When you remove the energy of anything broken from your life, you can start to become whole. That is worth more to you long term than the emotional connection to the fish.

❤ Lighting

Blown bulbs, damaged or flickering lights are telling you something is unsettled in that area of your life. Replace them as soon as they blow, and if it keeps happening get the electrical connection checked.

If bulbs fail regularly in your home, but there is no electrical reason for it to happen, you are probably experiencing exhaustion, overwhelm or tension and frayed tempers. Look for the cause and be kind to yourself.

❤ Plants

Traditionally Feng Shui recommends healthy plants with rounded leaves. The majority of books will suggest you avoid anything spiky because the spikes cut into your energy, leaving you feeling drained and out of sorts. Even if you have to part with your ancient yucca, there are still plenty of lush, vibrant options to choose from.

But at this stage, as you're simply looking around your home, look for any unhealthy, dead or gasping-its-last-breath plant. Its dying energy is not going to be doing you any favours.

Incidentally, if you keep an Aloe Vera on the kitchen windowsill to actively deal with burns, that's fine. If you keep it in your relationship gua, you might find things don't run too smoothly with the people you love.

💗　Use of rooms

All rooms in your home need to be regularly refreshed and opened up to allow Chi or life force into every part of your bagua. If you have a small home and use every bit of it, that's great. For those people who close the door on the dining room or a guest room and don't open it for months at a time, please make a point of getting in there at least once a week – even if it's just to wander in and open the window for a few minutes.

One lady with a particularly large house sends her young children to run around every room on a Saturday morning. They turn it into a game, and the laughter bounces off the walls, boosting the energy and improving the vibe.

Junk Rooms – can I just ask you why? Aside from the financial implications of keeping a junk room (which we will get into later), why would you dump a whole load of unused stuff in your space?

One newly married couple used their dining room to store everything they hadn't got around to dealing with since they moved into a big new property. They were doing OK in most areas of their life and were deeply in love, but the money wasn't coming in as it had done previously, creating a little tension in paradise. It was a big financial decision to call me in, and the husband wasn't convinced.

As we took all the boxes from the room, reviewed the contents and discussed the energy of the art, sculptures and horror movie posters, the couple decided to ditch almost everything. Within an hour the dining room was usable, the table laid, and that evening the couple sat down to eat at their table, boosting the Chi energy in the room and enjoying real conversation instead of taking supper in front of the TV.

The next time I worked with them, the husband was completely engaged and said he couldn't understand why it had taken them so long to sort out their home.

It's so important to keep Chi energy circulating, so there is no risk of you or your life stagnating. If you experience illness, throw open the windows and make a point of ensuring the Chi can flow all around your house, and there are no 'stuck' areas of dormant energy.

❤ Cupboards and storage

It is so very easy to bung a load of stuff into a cupboard and forget about it. Do you even know what's in there?

Look at the position of the cupboard on your bagua and identify which gua it sits in both for the whole home and the individual room. What is going on in those parts of your life?

And you know, none of us want our world falling down around us, so if when you open a cupboard you expect everything to fall out on you, it's time to get a grip on that area of your life too.

Tilly had a huge cupboard in the Fame and Recognition area of her home. She was a freelance teacher and very sporty, so the cupboard was full of equipment, boxes unopened since she'd moved in and her suitcases, as well as the domestic goddess stuff like the ironing board, vacuum and airers.

Tilly's work diary was ticking over, but she had quiet times when no one booked her. She wanted to do something to fill the gaps and took on a sideline which needed even more storage. Before she knew it, racks of stock had overflowed into her bedroom. Tilly was having problems sleeping, leading to a low mood and she never really relaxed. Although Tilly wanted to date, she knew she wouldn't feel comfortable inviting anyone back.

As we pulled everything out of the big cupboard on a damp November day, Tilly realised most of the things hadn't been used for 20 years. Her fear of parting with them meant she carried them from place to place whenever she changed city or country.

With a combination of donation, recycling and dumping, Tilly recovered more than half of the cupboard. This gave her space to store everything connected to her new sideline.

As we closed the door, she received a text from a potential new client who had noticed her advertising for the first time that day. He was followed by several new clients which meant her traditionally quiet period around Christmas was busier than ever before. For once, Tilly could relax and enjoy the time without worrying about cash flow.

And the best bit? Tilly met a lovely sporty guy who shares her love of the outdoors. It's all going well!

❤ Inherited or second hand/repurposed/vintage items

I'm a really big fan of recycling and repurposing furniture, especially the lovely solid wood stuff which can be painted or refurbished to look really special.

Most of the time the sanding, painting and cleaning process really freshens up the energy as well as the appearance, but I'd always suggest checking in with the energy because you often won't know where it has come from.

Right, 'checking in with the energy' you say, 'sounds a bit weird', I get that. So take a step back and go with me here. At some point in your life, you will have walked into a room and felt the hairs on your arms go up, goosebumps, even perhaps a heavy feeling seeming to press down on you.

That was your energy putting you on alert.

Hold that thought.

No matter how gorgeous a piece of furniture is, if it doesn't 'feel right' trust your instincts.

While I was with my ex, I upcycled a lovely drawer set. It had all the space he needed for his paperwork and looked great with our décor. The thing was, it never felt right.

Because I was stubborn and had put a lot of effort into beautifying it, I kept it. In fact, it stayed with me long after the end of the relationship – even Interiors Therapists have blind spots sometimes!

Ultimately when I moved to a new light-filled apartment, I really noticed the uncomfortable energy and let the drawers go. Despite losing excellent storage, I never missed them, even for a moment.

Second-hand mirrors are another item of furniture to be especially cautious about. They seem to take on energy more powerfully than other items. Perhaps it's because they see and reflect what goes on around them.

Working online with a lady in America, she pointed out an elegant full-length mirror. It had come from a yard sale, a total bargain and was the only long mirror she owned. Our work on her bedroom was going really well, and she was already feeling much lighter after only an hour or so, but her eyes kept travelling back to the mirror.

"It just feels so dark over there," she said, pointing at it. *"I'd never sensed it until now."*

I asked if she knew anything about the background of the mirror and her response gave us all the information we needed, *"Only that the lady who owned it committed suicide."*

Another client had a large stylish mirror in the entrance hall of her home. There was something creepy about it, and I asked if it had been in the house before she lived there. This was a wild suggestion because the house had been totally remodelled since the family moved in, but sure enough, the mirror had been in the house when they bought it.

I can't put my finger on exactly what the issue was, just that the mirror had reflected a lot of bad stuff. It was almost as though something scary was breathing malevolently just out of my eye line. A total goosebump moment!

So if you are buying or inheriting something which has previous owners, just give yourself a quiet moment and see how it feels to your energy.

If you bring something into your home and everything starts to go a little haywire, that's a good indicator of peculiar energy. It's not irretrievable, but you need to be sure it is really worth your time and effort to clean up the energy of the item.

The energy

Finally, for this section, we focus on the energy of the home itself.

- 💜 Do you feel welcome when you go home at night, or is your home indifferent or unfriendly?

- 💜 Are there areas of the home you find it difficult to relax in or choose to spend as little time there as you can?

- 💜 If you have pets, do they avoid certain places or hiss/ bark at an empty space for no obvious reason?

- 💜 Are there parts of the house where spiders are building cobwebs and nests regardless of the time of year?

- 💜 When friends visit, do they love to be there, or leave as quickly as they can?

Any of these signals or even a combination can indicate stagnation or disharmony in the energy of your home, and as you're already beginning to understand, your home reflects your life in ways you might never have imagined until now.

So by now you should have clarity about the impact of your possessions. Now it's time to move on to the next major stage.

CHAPTER 9

What does clutter give you?

Clutter is like energetic constipation in the home, if you let go, movement is inevitable.

The root of the word clutter is clot, and just as a blood clot prevents blood moving around the body, any clutter prevents energy moving around your home.

Clutter really is the bad fairy that just keeps on casting malicious spells.

Suzanne Roynon

A doctor friend of mine wishes he could prescribe Interiors Therapy and de-cluttering on the NHS. He believes it would slash the number of sickness certificates he has to write for patients with stress and cut anti-depressant prescriptions by more than half.

So before we get into the nitty-gritty of actually dealing with your stuff in the next chapter, these are just some of the symptoms you might be experiencing if you live in a home with too much stuff!

Mild Anxiety:

This can be triggered in a variety of ways. At the most simple level perhaps you can't find your passport, a particular shirt, those special earrings, an important document...

You invest so much time in looking for stuff, resenting your home, kids or partner that you can never just relax and enjoy life. In fact, life becomes a day-in-day-out drudge, but you keep plugging away, maybe with the help of medication, alcohol or over-eating, doing what you have to do to cope.

Overwhelm:

Everything seems to just get on top of you. At work, home, in your social or family life, financially or emotionally, it's all a struggle.

You could escape on the most incredible relaxing holiday or just a night out and feel fabulous, and then as soon as you return to your home, all the good feelings just evaporate.

Relationship problems:

A cluttered home is symptomatic of difficulties within the relationship. Everyone in the house is impacted by clutter, tempers fray, comments are misunderstood, and expectations aren't met. Couples are often aggrieved, numb to one another or ready to snap.

Living a simpler, clutter-free life gives you space to enjoy being together rather than blaming and resenting the person you love.

No Relationship at all:

It's exceptionally difficult to nurture a really special relationship when you cling to the past by holding on to mementoes, furniture, and photos from a past relationship. These things very effectively block the energy of a new relationship coming to you.

Some clutterbugs might date, but healthy relationships are elusive. People living a cluttered life often live alone but can transform their situation by taking control. After all, would you want to share your life with someone whose possessions are more important to them than you are?

Constant tiredness:

This is a self-perpetuating spiral. Clutter creates dust which causes breathing problems, interfering with sleep. A lack of sleep causes you to be tired and irritable. With long-term irritability comes negativity which seeps inexorably into every part of your life. This goes on to cause problems at work and home, perhaps leading to the loss of your job or your partner. This can result in financial difficulties and a fear of losing everything – so you cling on to what you have left, especially your clutter, and spiral down some more.

Weight gain:

Being surrounded by stuff depletes your energy, money, time and inclination to cook healthy food. You eat take out, ready meals, snacks, carbs, and wine, because it's just easier than trying to shop, cook and clear.

You're too tired to exercise. You're fed up and low in mood. Wham... You gain 20 lbs and feel worse!

Living in the past:

There are no two ways about it. If you spend a significant part of every day immersed in memories, it's going to be extremely difficult to find a way forward. Just by working your way through Chapter 8, you probably recognise a number of memory triggers around your home, which aren't helping you one little bit.

Think about Miss Havisham in Charles Dickens' *Great Expectations*. After she was jilted on her wedding day, her life stopped moving forward. She continued to wear her wedding dress and relived her loss each day for the rest of her life. She fed off the rejection and worse, she inflicted her sadness, vengeful thoughts and limiting beliefs on the people around her. Now, I'm not suggesting you've reached that extreme situation, but many people I've worked with were heading in that direction emotionally.

Living in the past doesn't need to be about the end of a relationship. It can just as easily reflect as an inability to deal with the property and possessions of deceased parents or children because everything contains a memory of childhood or a precious moment.

Any loss can shock your system into stasis, and the only person who can decide whether you choose to get life back into flow is you.

No matter how well-meaning your friends and family, you, yourself have to be willing to put the past behind you. This can only happen when the time is right for you. When you are ready, Interiors Therapy is the most wonderful way of putting the special memories safely in a box, parting with the depth of sadness and allowing the light of a brighter future to shine into the dark spaces of your home and heart.

And on that note, if you are reading this book because you have concerns about a parent, friend or someone you love, perhaps because their life is stuck and cluttered, before you reach breaking point, there is a way forward. You have to lead by example.

In the past I made the mistake of going into people's homes at the request of a third party. A sibling, partner or caring friend would pay for my service in order to get things going. What I quickly discovered is this causes embarrassment to the owner of the clutter, and drives a wedge between them and the person they love.

The thing is (and this is crucial to remember if you are reading this book because you want someone you love to deal with their stuff), there is a big difference between having quite a bit of clutter and descending into a hoarding mentality. Hoarding is a psychological issue which can have many triggers, and if you tell someone they are a 'hoarder,' even in jest, it can make them even more afraid to let go of unnecessary possessions.

So when I suggest you 'lead by example,' what I'm really saying is to deal with your own stuff first. There's an interesting energetic aspect to this. People have reported that when they start dealing with their possessions, perhaps they order a skip or clean out the garage, someone miles away has called them to say they spontaneously decided to clear their own stuff.

I've heard about this several times in my own practice, but it's also documented in other de-cluttering treatise and articles.

A really successful method I've seen employed is to invite the cluttered friend you are concerned about round for a coffee and 'be in the middle of sorting out.' They realise it's straightforward and even someone as fabulous as you are has some clutter. Often they go home empowered to do just a little bit, which gets the ball rolling.

Clutter is something which can be resolved through practical support and reassurance along with help to reorganise, but it's easy to slip back into a cluttered life if you don't complete the full process. I guess that's why new books about de-cluttering and tidying come out each year!

With Interiors Therapy, you go much deeper to identify the reasons behind keeping things and find ways to set a proactive course for the future. You have real reassurance your life will be significantly happier without the things you now regard as 'treasured possessions' but in a couple of weeks you will realise were easy to cast off.

Feeling stuck:

So you're trapped, with no energy and an unsatisfactory relationship situation. You don't feel at your best. You don't know which way to turn, and everything's getting on top of you.

All of the above can result in:

- ❤ Depression
- ❤ Relationship breakdown
- ❤ Weight gain
- ❤ Illness
- ❤ Insecurity
- ❤ Financial crisis
- ❤ Stagnation

Does that describe any part of your life?

Lynette had come out of a damaging marriage. Her weight had ballooned to over 17 stone which was way too much for her petite frame. Lynette's self-esteem was in pieces, and although the stress of the divorce had helped her lose a lot of weight (the 'broken-heart diet' can have its uses!), she was miserable.

Lynette got the opportunity to buy an apartment and asked me to help her move in. We got rid of everything which reminded her of her marriage, and as she settled into her fresh start, she regained her confidence and joined various social groups. The weight fell off her visibly, and through diet, exercise and determination, she reached her target weight and dress size 14. A couple of months later, Lynette asked me to help her make a Manifesto for Love™. But that's a story for later.

Clutter is the stuff we keep out of habit, fear, guilt or confusion, but it's those very things that prevent us from moving forward. It's not just about being weighed down (literally) by emotional baggage, or the negative connotations of clinging to the past, it's also about the physical impact of clutter on your space and the financial pressure on your wallet.

Let's look at that first. In any cluttered home, if you pay rent or a mortgage, your valuable income is being spent every single month on space to store things you do not need. It's just not a logical use of your hard-earned cash. Some people even pay for a lock-up unit when their clutter overflows their home.

Think about that for a moment. It simply doesn't make sense.

We are living in a time of such conspicuous consumption, and even with the words of Greta Thunberg ringing in their ears, girls will still insist on wearing a different outfit for every Instagram post. We are manipulated by Influencers and Corporations who want us to buy their latest product, wear fast fashion, own hundreds of pairs of uncomfortable shoes, and vote away human rights. While in some parts of the world, away from the gaze of social media, barefoot children work in sweatshops to make something we wear once and throw away.

It's time to get real about the things we buy, understand what we really 'need' to live a fulfilling life, and how to feel good about it along the way.

A hugely significant part of Interiors Therapy is to reframe your thinking. To be more aware of what and how much you buy, to reduce your consumption and only purchase items which you love, need and use – ultimately living a clearer, brighter, lighter life.

But now I'm preaching, so let's get back to it.

Statistics suggest, on average we use 20% of the clothes we have in our wardrobes 80% of the time. Leaving 80% gathering dust and taking up valuable room we could use for something we love more.

I suspect that's also the case for books, paperwork, vinyl, linen… but I'm getting ahead of myself.

Frankly, I'd rather have the space, so let's do something about that right now!

CHAPTER 10

Clear

By now, you have clarity, possibly for the first time, about the impact of your possessions and the effects of clutter on your home and lifestyle.

With the next stage, you make more room in your life, but it comes with a warning – if you only take half measures, you'll continue to feel stuck and suffocated.

So what do I mean by clear? This is about physically clearing things out. It's more than moving things from one room to another... this is about evicting anything holding you back from your life.

Most people tell me they feel obliged to keep belongings which aren't useful to them. Interiors Therapy challenges the empty justifications and excuses to look at things from a different perspective. If something isn't serving you, it has no place in your life.

But it's fair to say trying to clear on your own can be overwhelming, and it's tougher still when well-meaning friends or family offer to 'help'… then you have to deal with their emotional attachments to 'stuff' as well as your own… especially with gifts or inherited items.

The Facebook group www.facebook.com/interiorstherapy is a brilliant place to ask your questions, share your wins, connect with other readers on their own Interiors Therapy journey and get direct access to expert Interiors Therapists. You'll be surrounded by people who understand where you're coming from and want to help you succeed.

As you physically and emotionally clear everything which doesn't serve you, you open up space to welcome in anything that's missing.

Last minute preparation

You're going to need strong bin bags and sturdy boxes if you anticipate sending breakable or heavy items to charity, and a plan for where to donate, recycle, gift or dispose of your surplus possessions.

Find out which local charity stores will collect if you don't have access to a car and check when your local authority waste disposal site is open. It's going to be important to remove anything you decide is going out of your life just as quickly as you can.

Right, let's get started.

It's interesting to visit the homes of singletons who tell me they long to welcome a partner into their lives, but every drawer and closet is crammed with stuff – there's no room to invite in new romance, even when it comes knocking at the door.

For this reason, on most Interiors Therapy consultations, once we've reviewed the art, sculpture, ornaments and Feng Shui areas, the place we start work is the main bedroom.

As they start to work through their clothes, clients realise to their horror that they've spent hundreds, even thousands of pounds, euros or dollars on items they have no intention of wearing again or still have their store tags.

I worked on the south coast with Sarah, a well-dressed, down to earth senior manager with a luxurious apartment in a prime seafront location. She had a clearly stated goal for her Interiors Therapy. She was ready to fall in love. Sarah had focused 25 years on her career and never made time or space to meet a partner. She knew if she didn't do something about her surroundings, nothing would change.

My first impression of the apartment was of 1920s glamour. It really looked the part, and aside from a slight overload of photos and ornaments on side tables, it was very chic.

As we walked into the bedroom and she opened the wardrobe doors, I remember Sarah's words very clearly, *"Brace yourself, love."*

Oh boy! The built-in wardrobe was over 5 metres long, well equipped with rails and deep shelving. It was rammed so tightly the coat hangers were distorted out of shape and pulling anything out risked a small avalanche. At the bottom were over 100 pairs of shoes, boots and trainers, and in the top cupboards, Sarah kept three large crates of handbags and two tubs of scarves. In addition, foldable items were kept in the two large sets of drawers and the under-bed storage.

Here was a lady who loved clothes and was always able to put a great outfit together.

Sarah was hyper-motivated to clear anything holding her back, but even so, it took a full day to work through her clothes. Once she had identified everything she wanted to keep, we rearranged the wardrobe to suit Sarah's lifestyle, with two separate sections for 'work' and 'leisure'. The handbags were unpacked onto the shelf in shade sequence and the scarves colour-coordinated across three drawers, so she knew exactly what she had and where to find it.

On completion, Sarah had cleared almost half of the wardrobe space and even had spare drawers. The local charity store sent a truck for the bags. With plenty of space to share, it was no surprise when Sarah called to say she had met a lovely guy. They have just celebrated their second anniversary.

Begin with the wardrobe

In the majority of cases, the best place to start identifying clutter is, as Sarah found, the wardrobe. I describe it as 'honing your clutter muscle'.

It's usually possible to identify a selection of items you haven't worn and can't imagine yourself ever putting on again. Those are the easy wins, just put them straight on the 'to go' pile.

Then as you review the rest of the items these questions can be useful,

What is my first thought when I pick this up?

The most mundane items around your home can trigger memories, and it's no different with clothes. Some of the most delicious reminders and a few heartbreaking ones come at this stage.

"I wore this suit to my son's graduation. He picked it out for me and I've never felt so fine as I did that day."

"This is the T-shirt I wore the day my baby was born. It's old, but I love it so much. I feel happy whenever I wear it."

"It's a bridesmaid dress – I looked like a moose."

"This is such an expensive coat, and I used to love it, but I was wearing it when my wife told me she was leaving and that's always the first thing I think about when I take it off the hanger."

"My boyfriend hates this one."

"It's my school blazer; I'm 28!"

"These are my late wife's clothes. I can't bear to think of anyone else wearing them, so I kept them all."

"This is all maternity wear. The kids are in their teens."

"The shoes are designer, so beautiful and crippling to wear. I can't even walk to the car in them."

Those are just a few of the comments I've heard in the process of people reviewing their wardrobes. What it boils down to essentially is:

Do I feel good when I wear this?

Does it remind me of a sad, frightening or upsetting time in my life?

Am I keeping it because I feel obliged to?

Have I received mean or snide comments on my appearance in this?

When will I wear it next?

Does it fit?

Is it in good condition?

By answering these questions, you'll know if you want to keep it.

Fat clothes/thin clothes

Part of Sarah's wardrobe problem related to her keeping clothes from a time when she had been significantly larger. She kept what she termed her 'fat' clothes 'just in case'.

If you hear yourself saying you are keeping something *'just in case,'* that's a great big alarm bell ringing loudly – listen to it!

I asked Sarah if she planned to regain the weight, and she was horrified. *"Why would I do that?"* she asked?

"I don't know, Sarah, but as you've kept the clothes all this time you are evidently expecting to need them!"

The 'fat' clothes were an easy win. It gets a little more challenging when you consider the 'thin' clothes you have outgrown or the spontaneous purchases which you've convinced yourself will 'fit beautifully' once you've lost a couple of kilos.

It's not unusual for a lady to have clothes from size 10-18 in her wardrobe or a man to retain his tight jeans from his early 30s alongside the 'Jeremy Clarkson style comfort fit' pairs. Perhaps you could say it's a way of covering all bases, but in my experience, the people who do this have an underlying unhappiness with their weight and yoyo in the vain hope of getting back to their old size.

Keeping the 'thin' clothes or outfits designed for a much younger person is a self-critical reminder each time you open the closet that you are older and perhaps not feeling you are in the greatest shape.

Men and women describe feeling miserable and even guilty when they see clothes they can't wear any more. Still, they hold onto them out of habit or a vain hope that at some indefinable point in the future, they will wear them again.

It indicates an entrenched belief you won't be able to afford clothes if you do lose weight.

My view is that you keep the clothes which fit you now and release the rest. Anything too large or too small is blocking your energy and keeping you stuck in a place you'd rather not be.

If you anticipate losing weight (or gaining weight if that's the healthy option for you), then you can look forward to investing in clothes which really suit the 'new improved you' rather than swilling about in something you've had gathering dust in your wardrobe for years.

I think you deserve that, don't you?

Right, so before you start replacing the clothes you really love into your drawers, wardrobes and cupboards, give the insides a wipe to clear any dust and freshen up the space. Wooden furniture will often respond really well to a decent polish, and it will feel delicious when you open the door next time.

Clearing the Clutter

So what is clutter exactly? Put bluntly; clutter is anything you don't love, use or need.

The first question to ask yourself is:

Does it serve me now, and will it serve me in the future?

Or put more simply,

Do I love it, need it or use it?

We live in a culture which regards owning a multitude of possessions as evidence of success. We make excuses for buying and holding onto 'stuff' which neither supports or serves us because there is an expectation we will do so. These are the areas where clutter most frequently starts to build up:

- Clothes and shoes
- Books
- CDs/DVDs/Games
- Collections
- Gadgets/Technology
- Furniture
- Paperwork
- Sport/hobby equipment
- Photos
- Gifts

This is just the beginning.

Clothes and shoes

The majority of wardrobes I see when I visit clients are full to bursting, sometimes quite literally as back panels are pushed out of line by clothes being shoved against them.

Wardrobes are designed to protect and care for your clothes. It is not a competition to see how many hangers you can ram in before the rail collapses or the hangers are distorted out of shape. Nor is it essential to have suitcases full of unworn items stacked on top of your wardrobe. Clothes are easily damaged in this environment, and even if you can find the particular item you want to wear, it is likely to be crumpled or musty.

This category also includes:

- ❤ Over spilling cupboards

- ❤ Piles on surfaces and floors in the bedroom

- ❤ Racks, baskets, boxes and piles of jumbled shoes looking unloved by the door

- ❤ Things which never make it out of the bottom of the laundry basket

If the clothes you have invested in are unloved and unworn, they are taking up valuable space you pay for each month through rent or a mortgage.

The same scenario works for drawers. One client had so many clothes that there simply wasn't storage space in his bedroom to cope with them all. He had no idea what he owned. We gathered every item and checked each for wearability before folding and sorting into piles on the bed. He owned 79 pairs of socks, 42 white T-shirts, and over 60 work shirts. He explained that actually he hadn't worn a formal shirt to work for over 3 years. With support, he culled his clothes to a manageable level, selecting his favourite items to keep, and sending the rest to charity.

Books, books, books

Books are one of those items which people age 30+ struggle to part with. If you look honestly at your bookshelves, how many of the volumes will you actually read again? How many are unread? How long would it take you to read every book you own?

As I write this book, I am working with a lady who has always wanted a library. She envisions a beautiful room with elegant wooden shelving, stacked from floor to ceiling with books, even a ladder on a rail to enable her to reach the highest points in the space. For this reason, she hangs on to books in which she has no real interest but "will need books to put on the library shelves." In the meantime, her books are stored in boxes, double-layered on buckling bookshelves and taking up vast amounts of space in her garage. She can't find the books she actually wants to read because they are invisible amongst the haphazard 'library,' so she invests in a second copy rather than hunt them down.

Of course, the books in the garage and those spilling out into a shed, are deteriorating. The yellowed, curled pages, mildew, musty smell and brown spots on the pages mean they will never be welcome additions to any library.

I regard this as 'death by neglect'. People cling on to items they know they don't need or have space for in their homes, but they surmise they might just want them at some indeterminate time in the future. Rather than pass them on to be used by others, they keep them until a combination of dust, damp, and mouse attack means the only option is to dump or burn them – such a waste of valuable resources.

Reference books, often dating back to university or past study interests, course workbooks and textbooks connected to continuing professional development tend to stay on the shelf 'just in case'. The thing is, unless you are actually using them, they are taking space for oxygen and energy you could use for something more interesting. Ask yourself honestly whether the content of those books is helpful to you in your life and career now.

Paperback novels, unless they are your 'go-to' classics, are often read once and then consigned to a shelf – let them go! Keep only the books which you pick up over and over again. The rest can be replaced for pennies online if you find you need them... Which you probably won't!

Gadgets and Technology

Do you even own a CD or DVD player? When did you last listen to a CD or watch a DVD? These are an easy win – ditch any music you don't love and download the rest to your digital storage.

Games go out of date incredibly quickly, and between Amazon and Netflix you can find all the films you want on demand and not have to store hard copies.

Bread makers, old mobile phones and laptops, pasta makers, specialist baking equipment, hairdryers, straighteners... you get the idea. Anything you haven't used in the last year has no place in your home. Don't hold on to things 'just in case' or because you dream of being a domestic god or goddess. When the time comes, treat yourself to something new!

Furniture

Brace yourself, some of what follows will feel extreme, but trust me, I'm suggesting this for your own good.

If you have furniture, home décor items or artwork which remind you of a past love, perhaps because you chose it together or it was something they particularly treasured, then it has no place in your life. Why? Because like every other subconscious trigger, each time you see it, a tiny electrical connection activates a memory in your brain and generates negativity. After a while, you won't notice it anymore, but it will still be there niggling away inside you.

One client invited me to his post-divorce home. The place was a jumble of mismatched furniture jam-packed into a much smaller space than it had been designed for. I asked him about each item. Disturbingly, most explanations began with *"well my wife wanted that, so I kept it."* or *"it belonged to my wife's grandmother."* My client believed he had achieved some form of revenge on his ex-wife by keeping things which were precious to her. In fact, he was sending negativity to his brain each time he looked around his home and had surrounded himself with sour energy which impacted every part of his existence. No wonder he hated it there.

He was living in a place of emotional and financial lack. The marriage had ended despite his best efforts, and he was afraid to lose anything more. Despite realising the furniture he was keeping was preventing him from moving forward, he struggled to part with it. Eventually, he gave his ex-wife the option to have the furniture and then disposed of the remaining trigger items. Only then was he able to move forward in a healthy way.

Marital bed – this above all items is imbued with the energy of your former spouse or partner. Sexual energy remains a potent force long after a relationship has ended. Equally, the residual energy of pain, resentment and high emotion created by the end of a relationship lingers in the very fabric of the bed. As an absolute minimum, change the mattress at the end of a significant relationship, but ideally change the whole bed because the frame and the base will still retain damaging energy. Start a new relationship afresh and if you hit a rough patch with your new partner and come through it, consider replacing the mattress to symbolise putting the past behind you.

I cannot tell you how many people resist getting rid of the marital bed. *"Oh, I don't believe in the whole energy thing."* or *"We only shared it for a short time,"* are frequent justifications for keeping a bed.

Amoura kept her former marital bed for eight years. Remember, a good Interiors Therapist can only open your eyes to the impact of the items you hold on to. You alone can make the decision to let them go.

Even if it is blatantly obvious that a particular possession is causing problems for you right now, if you choose to keep it, don't be surprised if you keep going around in the same circles!

For Amoura, fear of lack was a big factor. Despite her large house and opulent lifestyle, the fear manifested itself in all kinds of ways and made everything a struggle for her. She kept the bed and several negative photos taken by her ex-husband because she looked great, and they reminded her of a time when she was happy and loved. At the same time, she was hurt when friendships withered, felt constantly let down by her children and family, and saw dating as a waste of time because no one measured up to the unavailable man she had a big crush on and regarded as her soulmate. Amoura spent a lot of time complaining, almost seeking out things to moan about… so the Law of Attraction gave her exactly what she was creating – more reasons to be unhappy.

Amoura had cleared massive amounts of clutter, lost weight, found new hobbies, joined a theatre group, got a fantastic new job. She could feel the transformation happening around her but could not see that clinging to the past with these last few items was actively preventing a new relationship from coming into her life.

Out of the blue, Amoura decided to buy a new bed and took advantage of the end of summer sales to invest in something really special. She dismantled her old bed and put it outside the house to be collected. Within 12 hours she received a text from an old flame inviting her out for brunch and later the same day was asked out by a guy at her gym and then by another in a Pilates class… But as Amoura told me on the phone, *"That's just coincidence, right?"*

Paperwork

If you hoard old bills, warranties, receipts, newspapers, magazines, birthday and condolence cards, lecture and seminar notes, how are they serving you?

Keep your tax information as required by law and if you don't need them for your taxes, retain only the most recent power/phone /pension/bank statements.

If you haven't referred back to conference or seminar notes since the event, they have become clutter – use them or lose them!

If you see something in a magazine and want to refer back to it, tear it out and put it in a file dedicated to articles you want to keep – then when you have finished with the magazine, pass it on to someone who will enjoy it or recycle it. There really is no value in creating a stack of newspapers or magazines and pretending that you are going to read them – you won't. So do yourself a favour and recycle them now without allowing them to drain any more of your energy.

Keep only the cards and letters which contain precious messages from loved ones and those which make you feel good, but don't hoard every card for the sake of it. You do not need to be reminded about who sent you a birthday card last year, and if a letter is just an update, why hold on to it? It simply does not matter. Condolence cards are a comfort in the first weeks after a loss, but then become a painful reminder in themselves. Consider carefully why you are keeping them; are they adding anything to your life?

Never, *but never*, hold on to cards or letters from a former partner or lover. By keeping them, you are allowing their energy to have power over you and prevent you from moving forward. They will not bring the partner back, but they will damage or even prevent any new relationship from developing in a healthy and happy way.

Hobbies and crafts

It's easy to buy a load of equipment in the first burst of enthusiasm for a new hobby. Then you stop doing it, and the riding hat, sailing gear, golf clubs, ice skates, Swiss ball or triathlon bike become clutter.

If you haven't used the equipment for over a year and have no plans to do so, why is it taking space in your home?

Do you really need the sewing machine you never used, the stack of jigsaws you've already accomplished, the sailing gear from 15 years ago when you were 3 stone lighter? If you aren't using it, it's clutter – simple!

One client, Jessie, invited me to her new apartment. She explained that life was significantly better since we had worked together. She had cleared her clutter. She was dating, work was good, she was mostly happy, but something felt 'not quite right'.

The new place was a huge improvement on her previous home. We moved some items around to enhance her Feng Shui, but really there was very little clutter to worry about. The only thing which felt out of place was the bike she kept in the hallway. Now Jessie doesn't have a car, so I assumed the bike was essential to her... wrong! As we surveyed the newly tweaked and tidied apartment, I asked whether there was a shed or bike store where she might consider putting the bike instead.

"I never use it, in fact, it belonged to the ex-girlfriend of my ex-boyfriend, and he gave it to me…"

Cue the sound of a thousand pennies dropping. *"I can't believe I've kept it,"* she said, *"It's going right now."*

Jessie put a note on the bike offering it free to a good home, left it outside her apartment and by the time she returned from a shopping trip it had gone. In one gesture she cleared a damaging piece of clutter from her life and did a Random Act of Kindness which provided someone with a new bike.

Photos

Are you still holding onto photos of your ex or your wedding album after the marriage ended? Every image and memory of a former partner, whether physical or online, is holding you back from the loving relationship you deserve.

One guy kept his wedding album in his attic even though his marriage had ended acrimoniously twelve years earlier. He justified this by saying the album included photos of relatives. He could not conceive of removing images of his family from the expensive album, so he insisted on keeping the whole thing. When he moved in with a new girlfriend, she refused to have it in the house, so instead of dealing with it, he stored it in his parent's attic. Hardly a vote of confidence in his new romance! Inevitably the relationship foundered. The album is probably still in situ, causing disharmony in each subsequent relationship he begins.

Ask yourself whether you really want the ghosts of relationships past being a constant presence in your new life. Would you want your new partner's ex-lover hanging around? No, I don't suppose you would. So why do you allow the energy of your ex-partner(s) to control the life you have now?

But I'm keeping them for the children...

If you are keeping wedding photos to pass on to children of the marriage, select one or two happy photos and put them in a special box or file which belongs to the child. Then give the rest to your ex if you believe they would want them, or preferably discard them.

It might feel uncomfortable at first, but as you cut the emotional ties to ex-partners, you are liberated from the old relationship and open to something new.

Also consider the packets of photos or albums you might have inherited from parents or those endless pictures of views which seemed so beautiful at the time, but now you struggle to remember where the photo was taken. Keep only the ones you truly treasure and genuinely add to your life. The rest are clutter and have no place in your home.

Digital photos are also clutter. It's so easy now to download hundreds of photos and leave them festering on your laptop. Go through the photos as you download them, keep only the best and ditch the blurred, badly composed or bad memory triggering images. That way, whenever you look at your pictures, you will only see those which boost your energy and make you feel good.

Don't be the person who keeps photos of all the people you've dated, or the home you lost in the divorce on your phone to show potential new partners (yes, this really does happen!); each image is draining the good stuff away from you.

Gifts

We've all received gifts we dislike. Each time you see them, they subconsciously impact on your wellbeing. The great news is that you don't have to keep them or allow them to clutter your life!

With a tiny shift in mindset, you can appreciate the generosity of the giver and then re-gift or donate with a clear conscience.

The things we surround ourselves with represent what we want in our lives. Sometimes well-meaning friends or relatives notice two penguins in your home, and suddenly every birthday you receive another penguin because people think you really like them and would cherish more. Before you know it, you have a colony of penguins peering at you from every nook and cranny.

The Pig Collection – a curly cautionary tale

A lady of my acquaintance had a large collection of pigs. China pigs, pigs in pictures, on tea-towels, even those kitsch flying pigs for the wall. Her pigs lived at her mother's house until, after a short courtship, the lady married the man of her dreams, a high flying, fit and sporty executive.

The lady moved her possessions into the new marital home and spread her pig collection about the place. They featured on tea caddies, trays and mugs. Their ceramic porcine sty-mates gambolled about the couple's home with gay abandon. No surface or wall was untroubled by the presence of a pig.

The sporty executive became a sofa slouch, lying in front of the TV in his piggy boxer shorts, eating and drinking to excess. He gained weight, became porky and lost his motivation, preferring to watch sport on TV than actually get involved. Their relationship deteriorated into arguments and resentment, with the man often being described as 'a pig' by his wife. Less than a year after their wedding the couple parted.

When the lady moved out, she took her pigs with her. The man regained his motivation and squeezed himself into Lycra and back onto his bike. A few years later he met a beautiful divorcee and they married. Their home is full of kids, dogs and love. There are no pigs.

Consider the impact of collections... pigs, cats, crystals, china figurines, magazines, comics, themed items, teddy bears... What are they saying about you?

Clearing the clutter throughout your home, either one room at a time or by deciding just to 'go for it' and starting at the top and working down like a whirlwind through every space, cupboard, drawer and cranny until the only things which remain are those you love, use and need will have a dramatic and positive impact on your life. You can't help but get a fresh start.

Yes, it is an investment in your time and energy. Yes, sometimes it feels overwhelming and unexpected memories tumble over you with waves of emotion, pain and heartbreak. Those are your motivators to part with the things causing you that hurt. You need never experience it again.

Once the first sweep of your home has been completed, you will already be feeling lighter, brighter and more able to move forward. Life will start to change around you; new people will turn up. Unhelpful people may disappear or just not matter anymore. Your attitude to life will change, and you may find yourself able to make huge life decisions because at last, you have some clarity. You will see beyond the stagnation which has been holding you back and realise you have been in a cocoon for years. Now you can enjoy a fresh start.

You'll find once you get into the habit of clearing things which don't serve you, you have a lower tolerance for clutter in your life. Most of my clients acknowledge that when they are feeling trapped or frustrated, the first thing they do is look around their house for new clutter and get rid of it.

One lady summarised it like this,

"I cleared a little bit of stuff and felt better, so I stopped.

Then it crept back, and soon I was feeling sorry for myself again. I'd do a bit at a time but never completed it. When I asked for motivation in the Facebook group, everything changed.

In a couple of days, it was done. I invested in my fresh start, and life just gets more amazing each month.

Now I'm tuned in to my Interiors Therapy; I'm loving my life."

This chapter has given you an overview of places to look for clutter and a summary of how to deal with the sort of things you might find along the way.

I would love to be able to go into infinitely more detail, almost room by room as I do with my clients and Interiors Therapy Masterclass students, but you are an intelligent person, and you've got the drift now. If you have another hundred pages of information to wade through before you get started, you'll be exhausted before you open your first black bin liner.

I'm going to suggest you put the book down now and come up with a plan to work your way through your home and get the clearing stage completed. Once you've done that, you're going to have more time, more energy and life is just going to be easier all round!

When you've cleared everything that's going, and reached the stage of being ready to revitalise the energy of your home, I'll be waiting for you in the next chapter.

CHAPTER 11

Consolidate

You might have read other books about clutter and worked hard to get on top of it, tidying and sparking joy, only to find the clutter came back, possibly even worse than before. There is a reason for that!

> *Nature abhors a vacuum.*
>
> **Aristotle**

And if like me, you've tried Feng Shui without clearing extraneous stuff first, you might also have found it backfired on you. That's because Feng Shui magnifies anything around it – all I got was more irrelevant stuff and aggravation!

You see clearing your home without consolidating the energetic change or trying to implement change without making space for it means you go round in circles.

Consolidation is an essential part of the process to cleanse the last of the negativity and prepare your home for your new life – the life you truly want to be living.

Steps to consolidation

The options available to you here are many, but the outcome should always be to successfully replace the negative stagnant energy you've evicted from your home with something infinitely more magnificent.

Before we get into the various methods, walk around your home and reassure yourself that everything you can see on the walls and on display is something you:

Need

Use

Love

If you've done a great job with your clearing, everything in your home should now have a place and purpose. Nothing you see should give you a sensation of sadness, doubt, or any other form of low-level emotional response.

Still check again that your art, photos and decorative items are in positions which reflect the areas of the bagua in which they are placed. If you aren't sure, you can always ask a question in the Facebook group at www.Facebook.com/interiorstherapy

Now you know your possessions are finely tuned to you and your home, it's vital to make time to deal with the physical dust, grime and stickiness which comes as a by-product of both having lots of stuff sitting around and the upheaval of dealing with it all.

This, depending on how you look at it, can be a chore or, as I prefer to see it, a chance to show your home how much you love and appreciate the safety, relaxation and security it brings you.

Clean as though it's spring

If I'm honest, cleaning and housework are quite low on the list of things I enjoy doing. I know some people get the most enormous sense of satisfaction, and I guess I do once it's finished. However, I have to admit, if someone is around who can make the place sparkle the way I want it to, I happily hand the job over to them!

But this time round, now you've cleared lots of space it's going to be easier, and your home will respond really well. As part of the changes within yourself and your life, take this opportunity to get to know your home as never before. Cleanse the dust and debris of your past once and for all. It's a blessing for you and your home, and it's a good way to spot the places where cobwebs, and therefore stagnant energy, have been playing havoc with your energy until now.

If you've never really been taught how to spring clean a house, Mrs Hinch can show you everything you need to know and much more on her YouTube channel.

If you are fortunate enough to have someone to spring clean for you, engage with them and be unambiguous about the depth of clean you expect.

I've only ever found one person who would polish up our busy family home to the extent that the house would, almost audibly, breathe out and say, "Ahhh Sarah." So Sarah Crump, if you could be cloned a million times over, the world would sparkle just as much as you do!

But right now I'm living far away, and despite trying agencies and individuals, I haven't found anyone who measures up to Sarah's standards. It's easier just to get on with it myself, and because home is clutter-free, it's a relatively simple job. I do one room at a time, purely for the sense of achievement when it's completed. Find and use a sequence which works for you.

Move furniture away from the walls and get to all the corners, crevices and around the skirting boards. Clean the windows, the frames, the dusty bits around and behind the curtains.

Wipe down every bannister, cupboard, surface, door and frame. Clean your mirrors, so they reflect back the brightest, most radiant version of you.

Deal with the dust behind the TV, on the shelves, behind radiators and vents. Move the bed and get under and behind it with a vacuum cleaner. Wooden bed frames and headboards get especially dusty, so remember to polish them up.

Zap the kitchen to leave it glistening. Pull out the fridge and washing machine if you can. They get very icky underneath, behind and on top. Tackle the toaster and microwave, wipe out the cupboards and treat the oven to a refresh. Give bins a thorough going over inside and out.

Hit the bathrooms hard. Polish taps until they shine. Deal with limescale, grime, soap-scum and the dust which gathers around the bathtub, in corners and on windowsills.

Wash or vacuum all floors. Give rugs and doormats a deep clean.

Clean the door handles, the light switches and all the fittings. Check high-level lampshades for sneaky spider webs.

Vacuum the furniture and plump up the cushions. Dust ornamental items; polish the glass and frames of pictures.

Water and primp your houseplants, wiping any dusty residue from leaves and cutting away any dead bits.

If you own crystals, give them a warm bath and lay them out to dry – ideally in sunlight or under the moon to recharge them. Crystals soak up negative energy and then let it seep out into the environment, so it's always important to keep them positively charged.

Clean the inside and outside of your front door.

Make a note of any damage and repairs required and arrange to get them sorted out.

By now you'll probably be a hot, sweaty mess, but your home will be tingling with new fizzy energy.

OK, so stage one is complete. Your home is now fresh, optimistic and ready to support you.

This is where you start to pump in the good vibes to keep the energy high.

Let's revisit the Feng Shui bagua to remind you of the areas you are working with:

Western Feng Shui Bagua

Wealth and Blessings	Fame and Recognition	Relationships and Love
Family and Ancestors	Health and Wellbeing	Children/ Projects/ New Beginnings
Knowledge and Spirituality	Career and Life Path	Travel and Helpful Friends

Doorway

Feng Shui Enhancements for Love

We talked previously about the importance of pair energy for either inviting or supporting romance. Identify all of the relationship areas in your home, note the main one on your bagua, and also the individual relationship areas for each room.

With the exception of bathrooms and shower rooms, place something to enhance the love energy in each area.

Make sure it is something which chimes with you. Some people might be happy to fill their homes with statues, rose quartz, twee Dutch kissing couples, bamboo flutes, lucky Chinese cats and goddesses... others most certainly will not!

There is no one way to enhance your love energy – it is as unique as you are. So I'm going to offer some potential ideas, and you can pick and choose as you wish. For more in-depth symbology, check out my website at www.interiorstherapy.com for downloadable PDFs on a range of subjects including love.

Some of the basics might include:

A picture, sculpture or figurine of a couple. I'd always recommend they are: looking at each other; focused on their partner; happy rather than miserable; the physical combination you desire; facing towards you rather than turned away from you or each other.

The ideal couple imagery is pretty hard to find, but they are out there if you look hard enough.

If you have a romantic partner already, enhance the energy in your bedroom by including a beautiful, happy photo of the two of you together. No children, no parents or friends, just you two.

Some people prefer to be a little less obvious and might choose a design featuring other kinds of couples. I've known clients choose cats, penguins, rabbits, swans and ducks, amongst others. I think the strangest was two coiled snakes, but that didn't end well, so I'd avoid that unless your dream partner has a passion for reptiles.

I'd also steer clear of anything featuring water. Water is known for triggering emotional outbursts, and in the areas dedicated to love, you'll want to be wary of tears and tantrums. The pictures of couples walking away from you into the sunset might look great initially, but when you experience your relationship going the same way, you might see things differently.

In any relationship area, think about using anything decorative in twos – two candlesticks, vases, crystals, plants, elephants (facing one another obviously). Avoid solitary items and especially photos of you on your own – regardless of how stunning you looked that day.

If it's new love you are interested in, consider putting white flowers and a picture of a couple holding hands and walking towards you into the area dedicated to new beginnings. In Western Feng Shui, white flowers symbolise a fresh start.

Main bedroom

Personally, I always encourage my clients to boost their bedroom for love, regardless of the area or gua it sits in. You can also boost the official gua energy but prioritise love in a healthy relationship in the room you sleep in because that's what you are reading this book for!

Pairs of lamps and matching bedside cabinets bring balance into a relationship.

Look closely at your imagery – you know this stuff now, but it's still easy to trip yourself up.

Allocate one side of the bed to your partner, even if you don't have one yet. Clear the cabinet on their side, so it's ready for them to use.

Consciously aim to sleep on 'your side' of the bed rather than being a starfish or bed hog. You are making space for your lover energetically, physically and emotionally in your life, so make room for them in your bed too.

While you are making space, be sure there is a drawer and some space in the wardrobe for their clothes. Leave a few empty hangers for them to use when they come into your life.

Mirrors are great in Feng Shui but have to be carefully positioned. Never have a mirror facing you at the end of a bed; it can cause energetic discomfort and drain you physically and emotionally. If you are stuck with mirrors reflecting you as you sleep (whoever thought mirrored wardrobes were a good idea?), try to cover them at night.

Think about the colours you use. I'm a great believer in keeping the space neutral and bringing in colour with bedlinen, cushions and art.

Traditionally pinks, whites, creams, golds and earth colours are recommended in a relationship area. Reds and deep pinks invoke passion but can interfere with sleep, so use them by all means, but if you find it difficult to rest, think about toning them down. I read long ago that peach and apricot can trigger infidelity, and from experience, I'm inclined to agree.

Strong colours aren't great for relaxing sleep. Blacks, deep purples, blues, yellows and greens can be an assault on the senses.

The saddest rooms tend to be the grey ones. Yes, I know it's terribly fashionable to have a house decorated from the front door to the luxury bed linen in fifty shades of grey, but my goodness it's depressing.

I'm always very blunt with clients in a grey home and ask them if they are feeling flat, listless, bored and de-motivated. So far, I've always been right. Interiors magazines and fashion have a lot to answer for.

Finally, if you have an ensuite, always keep the door closed and the lid down on the loo. If you are confident you won't leave the taps running, then plug the drain after use to stop good energy flowing away.

Routinely keep the bedroom fresh and clean. Make your bed as soon as you get up, so it welcomes you back in the evening.

Use your bedroom only for rest, romance and rejuvenation. No more work, laundry piles, exercise equipment or box-set bingeing. This is your sanctuary, treat it that way.

General points for other parts of the home

Always keep the lid down on any WC and ideally keep the bathroom door closed at all times. The bathroom is a place for waste to be washed away, and you don't want your good energy to slip out by accident.

Avoid decorating children's bedrooms with bright colours. Blues, reds, hot pinks, greens and yellows can be very overstimulating, which is something to bear in mind if your child does not sleep well.

Avoid placing a mirror opposite a door as you walk into a house or room. This symbolically reflects the good energy straight back out again.

Mirrors are used in Feng Shui to magnify and reflect, so positioning a pot of money or opulent fruit bowl in front of a mirror will increase your feeling of abundance. By placing a mirror behind a stove, you symbolically increase your abundance. This is also a good way of seeing who is coming up behind you as you cook!

There are helpful ideas and enhancements you can use in other areas of the home, and it's important that you maintain balance throughout the space, so do think about those areas too.

That being said, the practice of Feng Shui is extremely complex, and a specialist in the subject will have trained for many years under a Feng Shui Master. I always emphasise Interiors Therapy uses Feng Shui at a basic level to boost the energy within the bagua and help the home tune into your own beliefs and intentions as part of the bigger process.

Children, Projects and New Beginnings

This part of your home is all about the elements of your life where you want to make a fresh start. If you plan to move house and have an idea of the sort of home you are looking for, put an image of it here.

This is where you keep your new projects, plans and a vision board if you have one.

For anyone creative, this is a fantastic area to let the ideas flow and share your inspiration.

This is the place for photos of your children. I recommend regularly updating the pictures to avoid symbolically trapping children in childhood.

If you aim to start a family, images, art, a figurine of parent(s) with a child will work well in this space.

What new things or experiences do you want in your life? Perhaps you'd like to try skydiving, buy a new car or build a new business. Find a way of representing your dreams here, perhaps with photos or a written description of your intention. Is there a particular new job you aspire to? Keep a copy of the job description here.

White flowers are symbolic of new beginnings in Western Feng Shui, and I often give white orchids as gifts when I know friends want to start something new.

Health

This, above all areas, is a space to keep bright, neat, tidy and clean. Think carefully about what you put here. Homes often have storage cupboards in their centre areas which become dumping grounds for anything and everything. Stay on top of it. It's fine to have storage, as long as it's well organised and nothing is stagnating in there.

If the area is open, it's a perfect location for fresh flowers, pictures of you looking bright and healthy, and items you regard as exemplifying good health.

One lady keeps her vitamins and supplements here, and another lady, in her late 70s, has a skipping rope which she takes with her on her daily walk to the park.

Always avoid trip hazards and anything which could reflect death, injury or ill health. This is not the place to keep orders of service from funerals you have attended. If you must keep them, put them in your Family and Ancestors area.

If you have dead or dying plants or flowers, throw them out regardless of which area of the bagua they are sited in. They represent death and decay, which let's face it, isn't quite the energy you are after.

Family and Ancestors

This is the place for the photos of your parents, siblings, deceased relatives and for those you regard as family.

It's quite interesting when I visit very large homes with an enormous amount of space, the family photos are invariably displayed in this particular area.

This is where you might also keep details of a family tree, paintings of places you've lived previously, portraits of ancestors, or special items you have inherited.

However, this isn't the place for pictures of your children or grandchildren. They go in the 'New Beginnings' part of your home.

If you regard this area as the only safe space to place possessions reflecting your past, that will be a good start.

Knowledge and Spirituality

If you are studying, this is the most supportive place in the home to use as you learn. Keep your research and reference books in this area.

If you have a shrine, spiritual statues or books, this is the perfect spot for them. You might choose to do meditation, yoga or any other spiritual activity in this area.

It's an ideal place to curl up with a book or to encourage your children to do homework.

Of course, in Western Feng Shui, at least one of the baseline areas is going to feature the main door to your home.

If your Knowledge and Spirituality area is a tight space which includes your front door, aim to have a small bookshelf within the gua to boost the energy of knowledge within the home.

Career and Life Path

If there are particular pictures or objects which define the career you want for yourself, this is a great place to display them. One client keen to work for a particular media organisation put a copy of the company logo in a drawer and gained a contract position there soon afterwards.

One key element to remember about any images you choose for this area is to have movement in them. A boat in sail (ideally towards you), or horses cantering in your direction boost the Chi energy, however, a tidal wave is going to overwhelm you, so look carefully at what the image is saying to you. Anything facing out of the door could symbolically point the good energy away from you, so choose the image and direction carefully.

Water is a beneficial element in the career area, and a popular choice is to have an image of moving water, perhaps a waterfall or fast-flowing river. Again, fastflowing is good; flood is not. Find the balance.

Travel and Helpful Friends

We all need to have good friends and support around us, so this is the ideal place to put happy smiling images of your buddies.

You can also use this area for generating action from people you would like to help you in some way. If you want a fabulous cleaner to keep your home sparkling, or there is someone in your field who could really boost your profile, this is the place for written affirmations or photos of the useful person concerned to create the intention to make that happen.

One client felt her boss did not respect or understand her abilities. She created a 'job description' for the perfect manager and put it in an envelope in her helpful friends area. Within a couple of weeks, the company was taken over, and the client's new team leader recognised her skills and championed her progression and promotion within the organisation.

The travel element is fascinating, I think. I chatted with a young couple who, since their marriage, had enjoyed several cruise holidays.

"I can't understand it," said the wife, *"we've never chosen this type of holiday before, but we just keep booking them."*

When we checked that area of their bagua, which happened to be the downstairs loo, it was full of anchors and 'sail away with me' images they had been given on their wedding day. No wonder they spent so much time at sea!

It's important to set an intention when you include images with the plan of boosting your travel area, as I found to my cost! While I was living alone, I successfully generated visits to the US, Amsterdam, Paris, and many other wonderful places. However, when my daughter moved home for a short while, I obviously wasn't clear enough with the energy of our home. I'd put pictures of Venice, New York, and the Caribbean into my travel area, but when the opportunities arose, it was my daughter who travelled rather than me.

So as with anything you want to manifest into your life, be abundantly clear on your intention.

Wealth, Blessings, Abundance

This is an area which deserves a book in its own right, and a quick search on Google will find you a dozen or more on this very subject.

The wealth area is the place to display images which represent abundance to you.

The simplest way to activate an abundance area is to include an overflowing pot of money, ideally sitting on a mirror to effectively double the contents.

People attuned with the Law of Attraction might choose this space for a manifesting 'cheque from the universe' to draw large sums into their bank account.

Many cultures have gods and goddesses which represent wealth, for example, the Hindu goddess Lakshmi or the Roman goddesses Abundantia or Fortuna. You can also find crystals reputed to boost your income, citrine and jade are very popular but wash them regularly to keep their energy fresh.

I've seen boxes and pots in gold or silver metal used very effectively.

Oranges in a painting or fresh fruit in an opulent bowl.

You can also choose to place money plants here, along with images which depict what wealth means to you, jewellery, the yacht, the lifestyle.

One thing to bear in mind though is this is not the place to keep your accounts information if you have debts. Instead, keep the paperwork in the Family and Ancestors area, which represents the past rather than the present.

Fame and Recognition

This is the area representing what you want to be known for. Although we use the word 'fame,' that doesn't necessarily mean having your name emblazoned in lights or across the front of the newspaper. It's really about your reputation and how people see you.

Say you make amazing cakes. This is the place to put the pictures of the cakes you are most proud of – create an album and keep it here.

Perhaps you're a writer and want to be recognised. Put a copy of your book in this space to generate good energy around you and your creation.

Is there a word which exemplifies how you want to be seen? One client had been given a 'World's best mother' plaque by her children. Being a great mum was the only thing which mattered to her at that time, and her fame area was the perfect place for their gift.

For a petrolhead client, his pride and joy was the car he had restored and raced. The pictures of him with his car and with other racers were a source of constant joy.

Perhaps there is a particular award you would like to win? Find an image representing the award, and if you are tech savvy, mock-up a photo of you with the award and keep it in this area of your home to generate the positive energy around it.

This is also the place for budding television types to keep photos of BAFTAs, actors to have Golden Globes and athletes to aim for Olympic glory. You get the drift?

Some people seem to naturally use this space to place their marathon medals, pictures of them with celebrities, or to mark other achievements. They seem to know, without having any knowledge of Feng Shui, this is the ideal place to show what you are made of.

Whatever you choose to display in this area, make it positive!

Each area really is worthy of a book in its own right, and these are just hints about the enhancements or choices you could make to boost the energy within your Bagua. You can find additional information on my website and also in the myriads of books on Feng Shui.

The next stage comes only when your home is clean, the Feng Shui has been tweaked, and you are absolutely clear about the support you want from your home going forward.

Space Clearing

I love working with my clients on their Space Clearing Ceremony. We always devote at least half a day to the process and turn off all distractions to make it really special for them.

The process involves opening windows, so it pays to check the weather forecast in advance and choose a day when the weather is kind. It doesn't matter if it's cold, but a howling gale or vicious rainstorm would reduce the enjoyment quite considerably.

If you have kids, it's great to get them involved, but if you think anyone in your home might be unsupportive, arrange to do the ceremony when they are elsewhere.

You are going to need:

- ❤ Pen and paper
- ❤ Something to make a noise with. I usually clap my hands, but in a big house or for someone with rheumatism or arthritis, we find another method. One favorite is banging on a child's drum; another option could be a wooden spoon and a metal bowl or even a rainstick or rattle if you happen to have one.

❤ Salt – enough to run along the thresholds of all external doors.

❤ A smudging bundle or other suitable slow, light smoke producing option – white sage, lavender, dried herbs, incense. We want the smoke to waft throughout the home in gentle waves – not set off the smoke alarm!

❤ NB If smoke is simply not an option in your home, use a cleansing aromatherapy oil such as bergamot, lemon, frankincense, tea-tree or any of the other citrus scents in a mobile diffuser or in a jug of steaming water.

❤ A bell, tingshas or bright, beautiful music to fill the home with pure sound. I use a Tibetan bell, but I've also seen tuning forks, a xylophone, or even a steady 'OM' chant used for this stage.

You might also like to include fresh flowers, holy water, a spray containing spring water and aromatherapy oil or anything your cultural background uses to cleanse or as part of ceremonial activity. I choose not to use candles or incense sticks with clients anymore because of the risks involved in leaving them unattended, but I do light a pillar candle for my own space clearing ceremonies at home.

Step 1

Write a love letter to your home telling it how much you appreciate living there, the difference it makes to your life, how special it is to you. Tell it all the things you like about being there, how welcome you feel, and how happy it makes you to see the new space and light around you.

Even if you don't much like this house or you want to move away, find the things about your current home you can be grateful for.

Then explain what you want to draw into your life. Although this book is theoretically about love, that's just one part of a fulfilling life. So tell your home about your hopes for the next year or so, the places you want to visit, the job promotion or opportunities you want to come your way. Define your creativity or any other activity you love and achieve in. Tell your home about the wonderful friends, guests and experiences you want it to share with you. If you have goals set, include them. If you are speaking on behalf of babies and toddlers, add in your hopes for them.

Thank your home and sign your letter with love.

NB I've done this work very successfully with children aged about 5 years and upwards. They don't necessarily write things down, although the older they are, the more they can be encouraged to do so. The little ones normally listen to their parent(s)' love letter and then wriggle in excitement until they are allowed to thank their home and tell it what they would like.

When you (and everyone else involved) have your letter ready, create a 'base station' with your smudging kit, bells and anything else you feel drawn to use. Ideally, put your base as close to the front door as is practical, but it doesn't matter if you end up in the kitchen or another room.

If you have adjoining neighbours, it's a good time to pop round and say you'll be a little noisy for half an hour, but it won't be too long. You don't want irritated people banging on your door part way through your ceremony!

Open a window in every room. If possible, also leave the front and back doors open until after the smudging.

Draw a line of salt along the outside of all the exterior doors, including patio, French and back doors in addition to the front.

Step 2

Turn off all music, TV, noisy equipment like dishwashers and washing machines. Have the home as silent as you can.

Cover any food on kitchen surfaces and ideally put pets outside. Animals are very sensitive to shifts in energy, and the ceremony can be unsettling.

You're going to move around the house in a clockwise direction across all floors and into every room, clapping/making a banging or rattling noise from the top to the bottom of every corner in every room and along the walls in between them. Open the cupboards and make a noise in there too. Remember to get under the stairs, in the metre cupboard, wardrobes, cubby holes and anywhere else you can find.

This step is to wake and shake up any dormant energy which has managed to elude you so far. This is why it's important to have the windows open so the energy can escape and not just settle back in.

Sometimes you might feel a rush of something passing you on the way out of a door or window, it's fine. Pockets of energy can be small or large, and when the bigger ones go, they can leave with a whoosh and a slamming door (a bit like a stroppy teenager).

Now wash your hands and arms up to the elbows to rinse away any mucky energy.

Step 3

Back at your base station, light your smudging bundle or prepare hot water for your steam cure. (Saucepans or boiling water and scented oil are another variation here.)

Follow the same route around your home into all rooms on all floors. Waft the smudging smoke or scented steam into all the rooms and cupboards. Leave cupboard doors open if you can. This layer of the ceremony smokes out anything which managed to avoid the noise earlier.

As you finish step 3, the home should be feeling calm and almost have a sense of anticipation. Close all the windows and doors.

Step 4

Back at the base station, read your individual love letters aloud to the home. I always think saying things so they can be heard makes them all the more powerful.

If you are doing this with others, restrain yourself from interfering in anything your family say – you might well learn something amazing about them if you just listen and absorb rather than judging their language, speech or dreams.

If someone really doesn't want to read out loud, then ask them to read the letter to themselves. The important thing is to repeat the love for the home and desires for the future at an energetic level.

Step 5

When you have all said your piece, take the bell, tingshas, the music you have chosen or even just your OM if you prefer.

Take your third walk throughout your home. This time you are consciously feeling joy and delight in your space. As you ring the bells, never allowing the sound to die away, visualise each room being filled with bright white light, spreading and sparkling into every corner. If you aren't humming OM, then repeat 'Thank you home' or similar words which feel right to you over and over again as a mantra or affirmation until you have visited every room and cupboard and are back at your base.

Step 6

Take a moment to thank your home and your tools for being part of the Space Clearing Ceremony.

Leave the house for at least an hour for the energy to settle down. If you can, go for a walk and find the beauty around you, or maybe just hit a coffee shop and breathe in the aroma of the beans, that's fine too.

I normally find somewhere safe to set fire to my letter and allow it to go out into the energy of the world, but you can choose to keep it in your New Beginnings or even Helpful Friends area if you wish.

Step 7

When you return home, allow yourself time to adjust to the different energy. People describe their home glowing or feeling very bright and new. Others say they can hear faint music or pick up happy vibes.

Recognise and appreciate the fresh space around you.

In the next few hours and potentially the following day, you may feel floaty or a bit spaced out while your energy adjusts to the clear space. This is completely normal, just relax and let it happen.

PART III

Create

By this stage in the process, you've taken massive action. Your home is in alignment, opening the door to further success.

The only thing holding you back now is you!

Statistically, according to a range of academic studies, you are around 42% more likely to achieve your goal if it is written down. But you're an astonishing 87% more likely to reach it if it's in writing, you take action towards it, and you have accountability to someone else.

And that's what Create is all about. You make decisions about what you want and take action – you are reinforcing great new habits and transforming your life.

The Facebook group gives you an accountability group if you choose to use it, otherwise get your supportive friends on board to hold you to your commitment.

Joanna's Story

Joanna was well into her Interiors Therapy journey. Her house had been transformed, and she was already much happier in herself. She had started online dating and met a couple of guys.

After spending a lovely afternoon which had morphed into dinner with a date, she'd had a superb time but realised there was no spark. She wasn't sad though, instead, she was animated and happy to know there was someone 'out there' who really was almost everything she was looking for.

Joanna had been having so much fun, she missed her last train and had to wait for a bus instead. At the bus stop, she overheard some bikers chatting very positively about Hells Angels.

"Ah," thought Joanna, *"Perhaps what I need is a Hell's Angel."*

"If you'll budge over, ah can sit doon." said a man's voice above her. His accent wasn't local, a gentle burr suggesting he came from the Scottish borders.

Joanna did as asked and got drawn into a fun and animated conversation with the man before she looked into his handsome, bearded face then down at his clothes…

"I couldn't believe it, just one quick thought and this hunky Hell's Angel had materialised beside me!"

Sure enough, Joanna manifested a handsome, gentle Hell's Angel to chat to until her bus arrived. She never asked why he was at the bus stop. He simply waved her goodbye as the bus pulled out and then walked away!

Joanna's laughter tinkled around us as she told the story.

"I never realised I could do this so precisely," she said, *"Now I know I can ask for anything I want and it will come!"*

CHAPTER 12

Preparing to be loved

Now you have your house in order, let's take a look at you. The changes, big or small, are probably happening around you, but are you aware of them yet? Perhaps you're getting lucky breaks, a parking space or last-minute appointment. Maybe you've found money, won a prize, got a tax rebate, completed a task which has been hanging over you for longer than you can remember.

How do you feel about yourself now?

Start to really pay attention to what is happening in your life. Interiors Therapy can initiate energetic shifts which might take you in all sorts of unexpected directions or just make life flow in a different and ultimately more positive way.

Don't be surprised if some relationships dramatically transform for the better or when flaky, unhelpful people leave your life. This can include friends, colleagues, dodgy neighbours, even partners and spouses – especially if the relationship has been under pressure. Even if it hurts right now, trust that it's happened in your long-term best interest.

Be open to new opportunities, perhaps an unanticipated promotion or pay rise, receiving recognition for your efforts or clients seeking you out.

Of course, when you are ready and in the best place emotionally, you'll find you attract romantic interest from unexpected quarters, but don't rush this. Make your Manifesto for Love™ before racing headlong into anything new in the love department.

There is no set timescale, no defined list of outcomes you can expect. Every person experiences Interiors Therapy differently because everyone is unique and has a slightly different intention for the results they want to achieve.

Change your language and outlook

Do you recall my advice to Lisa back in Chapter 4 about changing the way she spoke and thought about people and situations?

I want to reiterate it here because this is really important. Be conscious at all times about the words you use. The more in tune you get with your energy (and Interiors Therapy is a huge part of this), the more powerful and adept you become at using the Law of Attraction. I'm going to go into a little more detail about the Law of Attraction later in this chapter, but for now, I want you to concentrate on your thoughts, words and deeds.

If you knew your words and thoughts would rebound on you somehow, would you still say them?

Well, if you regularly say, 'I love you', 'you're wonderful', 'thank you', or anything else which is positive or even just neutral or a statement of fact ... *("I'll have a cup of coffee please"* counts as neutral, *"the train is due now"* is a statement of fact). Then yes, I'm guessing you'd love to hear those words and feel the energy associated with them.

How do you feel if someone says, *'I hate you', 'you are pathetic', 'your product is worthless'*? Not so comfortable, huh?

So if you knew every time you said something cruel, trolled someone on Twitter, complained for the sake of complaining, spread some nasty gossip, moaned about something or someone who is doing their best to serve you, your comments would eat away at your own energy, creating more negativity around you, and generating more things to be unhappy or dissatisfied with... would you still do it?

Sadly, lots of people do. We all know the person or people so bitter and twisted that we grit our teeth when we have to spend time with them or even go out of our way to avoid contact. There is always something to complain about, some drama or reason for them to feel aggrieved and boy do they like to spread the misery around.

Some people seem to feed off low energy, and I'll let you into a secret, like a vampire, they will feed off you!

It's totally draining to be with a negative, whiny, whinging person; someone who is constantly expressing anger, distrust; or believes they are always the victim of circumstance. Every part of life becomes a struggle, the slightest hiccup will be taken as evidence the world is against them and they moan about anything and everything. Festering resentment is their baseline emotion. Understandably, in their company, you can almost feel the last dregs of happiness being sucked out of you, rather like a date with one of Harry Potter's dementors.

And guess what, remember the Law of Attraction says what you state, you create? Well those ultra-pessimistic people do just that, they create more destructive, depressing energy around them and more things to grizzle about.

I have first-hand knowledge of this – at various times in my life I have been that negative, drama dependent person and believe me, everything that could go wrong did so. In one job, I was known as 'Mrs Doom' and frankly, the label was uncomfortably accurate.

When I snapped out of it, whoosh! Everything changed, and I can assure you, it really can for you too.

Whether you are a Mr Misery or Ms Glum, or you have the misfortune of spending a lot of time with one, break free of the cheerless hold this destructive energy has over you.

It's not an overnight thing – be kind and ease yourself into it gently. Start with your regular critical thoughts and reframe them to positive statements:

'I feel fat.' – 'I prefer to weigh 65 kilos.'

'I hate my wrinkles.' – 'My face lights up when I smile.'

'I'm unlovable.' – 'When I love myself, everything else is a bonus.'

'The train is always late.' – 'Everything happens in perfect time for me.'

'I can't get a date.' – 'I have other options to enjoy.'

'People are so rude.' – 'I can surprise them with a smile and kind words.'

'No one appreciates me.' – 'What can I do to change my energy?'

Avoid tapping into someone else's drama

This can be small scale, like adding a critical comment to a social media thread, or always being on the receiving end of your Drama Queen friend's latest traumatic experience. Honestly, some people can create energetic havoc by their response to a store running out of milk, a delayed train or inconsiderate dog walker!

I want you to imagine each nasty comment, thought or word you make is like a little dagger point stabbing into you – because that's what you are doing to your energy and that of the people around you.

But if you avoid engaging with the critical comments, whining and grumbling, and think about something more proactive, it just brushes past you. Result!

Sometimes something really dreadful happens, a train crash, terrible accident or attack, it's hard to manage the feelings associated with it if you are engrossed in TV news or a social media thread. If I say 9/11, then your subconscious will immediately show you images from that heartbreaking day, and your mood will be dampened, if only for a moment.

Earlier, we talked about the power of images in Interiors Therapy and how life mirrors art and vice versa. Images are incredibly potent memory and emotional triggers. They are stored away in your subconscious to be pulled out whenever you think of the situation. The easiest way I find to manage this is to avoid TV news and newspapers altogether, and aim to block out news images on social media. That way, I don't store or connect images and emotions relating to things I can do nothing to fix. I listen to a couple of news bulletins each day to keep up with events, but rarely see images. I know what's going on without investing my energy or emotion in the visual intensity of the news story.

So even when someone close was involved in a traumatic incident, I chose not to watch the news or see any images of the location or people involved. My reaction was very detached, sending good vibes and positive energy to the people involved, but not engaging in the trauma of the images. By feeling love rather than fear, I prevented the incident from getting under my skin, and the detachment meant I could be more useful than I would have been had I allowed fear and hysteria to overtake me.

A note on malevolent thoughts

As you become more powerful, working with your thoughts and energy, you will see the impact of your energy showing up around you whether you think positively or negatively. While it doesn't quite give you superhero status, it does mean that you need to use your ability wisely.

I'm sure at one time or another you have been angry or hurt enough to think cruel thoughts about someone else or wished harm on them. The more energetically engaged you become, the more likely it is for your negative thoughts to cause actual physical damage to others. Be mindful and cautious whenever your temper flares and is targeted at a particular person.

Why is it important to remind you of this? Well, quite simply because, rather like a boomerang, the energy you send out will inevitably come back to you and often at double the intensity. While you might momentarily rejoice when the person you were angry with has some mishap, at some point in the not too distant future, that negative energy is going to come right back at you and cause you harm… Wham!

I can never reiterate these words from Mike Dooley enough; thoughts become things – choose the good ones.

Make a decision to love who you are

I'm sure you've heard the words 'you have to love yourself first.' I'd say that's the best advice anyone can ever receive if they want to fall in love in a balanced and life affirming way.

How can someone love you if you don't love yourself? Can you expect to understand the emotions, the need to nurture and support you deserve from a partner if you don't give it to the most important person in your own life – YOU?

And if you don't think you are worthy of love, why should anyone else want to invest their time in getting to know you?

So chew that over for a bit while you do this exercise:

♥ Exercise – What makes you loveable and a great catch?

Write down 25 reasons why you are the perfect romantic partner for a really special person.

Then if you can, to hold yourself accountable, call a trusted friend and tell them what you believe makes you worth looking for.

A touch on the Law of Attraction

What can I say about the Law of Attraction which you haven't seen or heard in any one of hundreds of books, TV shows, films and blogs on the subject?

This belief has been around for many thousands of years, and the suggestion is that the knowledge of the way in which the Law of Attraction works has been deliberately hidden from the masses until relatively recently. These are some of the more famous quotes about the Law of Attraction, and as you can see, it's not all new age 'woo woo' motivational speakers who believe in it. Both Buddha and the Bible get a look in, as do Albert Einstein (1879-1955) and Napoleon Hill (1883-1970).

Quotes

Ask and it will be given to you; seek and you will find; knock and the door will be opened to you. – Matthew 7.7, *the Bible.*

What you state, you create. – the wisdom of Abraham Hicks

If you see it in your mind, you will hold it in your hand. – Bob Proctor

Imagination is everything; it is the preview of life's coming attractions. – Albert Einstein

What you think, you become. What you feel, you attract. What you imagine, you create. – Buddha

Whatever the mind of man can conceive and believe, it can achieve. – Napoleon Hill

The reality you experience is a mirror image of your expectations. – Deepak Chopra

So what I've found is that it's relatively easy to get the Law of Attraction on side for simple things. Parking spaces are famously straightforward to accomplish and these days we have a great track record of making it easily onto trains, planes and boats when they should, by rights, have already departed.

Somehow, without really understanding what I was doing at the time, I managed to attract my dream home when we got married, and then a perfect cottage and garden after my divorce.

This was long before 'The Secret', and I had never heard of the Law of Attraction, so I was evidently tapping into something deep inside which I now understand was the Law of Attraction at work. Looking back, this involved identifying the property I really wanted and then imagining how it would be to live there, what I would do to the garden, how it would look inside. I would walk or drive past it regularly and say 'Hello'. Deep inside, I was certain the houses wanted to be mine, and ultimately they were.

Other Law of Attraction achievements included a free natural stone terrace, gifted and laid by a neighbour; meeting and falling in love with the man who was perfect for me at the time; getting my daughter into a fantastic school against all odds, and many more smaller, less significant 'wins'. Then years later, a flood which could have been seen as a disaster, gave an opportunity to remodel the house – literally within weeks of drawing the 'ideal layout' on the back of an envelope.

When I'd drawn my scruffy floor plan, I jumped up and illustrated to my partner where everything would be, laughing and waving my hands around exuberantly. I had no idea how we could pay for it, or remain living there while huge building work took place, I just defined how I would love our home to be and got on with my day.

When we woke up to a small lake of water surrounding and infiltrating the house, a freak event due to a blocked ditch on the adjacent farm, the momentary fear and upset drained away much more quickly than the water. The insurance company would cover the cost of accommodation for six months while the house dried out. All I had to do was take the settlement and remodel the house to my specifications. The Universe presented the way to make my plans come to life.

So what makes these things happen? Is it nothing more than coincidence, or can we truly attract the things, people, connections and situations we want into our lives?

Well I think it's more than coincidence that so many wonderful things happen when I'm feeling happy and in love with the world. I also believe that we are more likely to attract bad stuff if we focus on negativity.

If you get into a car when you are angry, you're statistically more likely to have an accident. But funnily enough, I've noticed that cars often fail even to start if someone is already in a bad mood. If you are stroppy or grouchy, then it's reasonable to expect things will get worse. I think that's because you create grumpy victim energy around you. If you complain or see a headline which annoys you, that tight feeling across your chest or in your gut could easily stay with you all day.

And you know this also goes for relationships – if you think your partner might leave you for someone else, you shift the energy in your relationship and create an open door for them to do so. If you expect them to behave badly or you feel jealousy, chances are they will ensure you have reason to do so.

So bearing all of this in mind, what simple steps can you take to implement the Law of Attraction?

Personally, I think it's all about the ACTION. Actively visualising what you want for yourself, how it will look and especially how it will feel. When I decided I would like a beautiful terrace in my garden, I saw myself sitting there with friends on a sunny day. I imagined the table, chairs and the aromatic flowers and shrubs in their pots on the terrace. I created the vision of relaxing in a shared hammock on the terrace and looking up at the starlit sky surrounded by the scent of jasmine, honeysuckle and stocks. What you state, you create! And I did.

So how come it's easy to manifest the things which don't really matter (OK, excluding the houses, but that was before I knew about the Law of Attraction), and yet it's so much more challenging to do the big stuff.

Well there is the answer in a nutshell – if you believe the big stuff is more challenging, it will be. And that's a limiting belief in its own right.

Essentially, the Law of Attraction is always working, whether you choose to believe in it or not. So on the basis of probability, I'd choose to focus on positive thoughts because anything else is just letting the bad stuff seep in.

Random Acts of Kindness

Random Acts of Kindness just spread joy. I love thinking about them, doing them and receiving them. Most cost nothing – holding a door open or smiling at a stranger. Offering to take a picture of a couple or family group so they can all be in the picture; sitting on the pavement to talk with a homeless person rather than just walking by. Letting a car out ahead of you at a junction or passing on a partially used parking voucher; inviting someone to jump ahead in the checkout queue, all create a good vibe.

Sometimes I'll send a handwritten card or letter complimenting a receptionist on her great customer service or thanking a particularly helpful sales assistant. Everyone loves a handwritten letter, and in these days of emails and texts, they stand out and are doubly appreciated.

I've bought up large bouquets of roses for pennies on the day after Valentines and walked through town gifting them to people I've never met. Left pot plants and flowers on the doorsteps of neighbours (even the unfriendly ones!), and returned a lost notebook to a man in Japan. It's all done anonymously with a little card saying, 'you've received a random act of kindness.' There is no expectation of reward; no one has a clue where it came from, and it feels great.

Of course, it's also lovely to do things for your friends, colleagues and family; but there's something really special about boosting positive energy around a stranger, and funnily enough, unexpectedly enjoyable things seem to happen for me afterwards.

There are endless lists on the internet to give you ideas for Random Acts of Kindness. Be inspired by them or make up your own. Anything and everything you do to infuse your life with positive energy is going to be a good thing for you and the people you love.

Be the best you

Some of the best advice I ever received was 'enjoy your single years'. The first time round, after my divorce in my late 20s/30s, I spent my single time angsting about being on my own. I must have been an absolute pain to everyone who knew me. Sorry folks!

Then at the point I realised I was having a whole lot of fun being able to do my thing without having to consider anyone else, the long-term relationship turned up. Although we had a reasonably balanced time for the first few years, I'd be fooling myself if I didn't acknowledge putting some of my own priorities on hold – permanently!

The next time round, now in my 50s, almost my first thought after closing the door on my ex was, 'Right, what have I been missing out on?'

I got back into hobbies I loved, returned to self-development, got back into what's now known as Interiors Therapy and formalised my qualifications.

I didn't really consider having a partner as essential to life. I just got on with enjoying it and had a lot of fun along the way.

When I realised my subconscious was encouraging me to focus on myself, I quite deliberately tweaked my Feng Shui to generate new friends, travel, adventure, and changing my career. The symbology which had bought my ex into my life was disposed of permanently.

Dancing gave me lots of human contact and affection. Believe me, a connected dance with someone (even a complete stranger) can be delicious!

My many new friends and the return of old friends who had been pushed away meant every weekend was full of laughter and excitement.

I started to travel abroad alone, visiting places and exploring them on my own terms. I read, learned, researched, studied and explored. It was inspiring to find out how far I could push my self-imposed boundaries.

Yes, I got asked out, quite a lot actually, but I'd spent so much time making Manifestos for Love™ with my friends, that my sense of the kind of person I wanted to date was very clearly defined. At that time, I rarely set foot in the circles where he was likely to be found, so instead of constantly looking for a date I did new things, met extraordinary people and pushed myself way out of my comfort zone. It was great!

In fact, when it came down to it, there wasn't really room for a romantic liaison, and that suited me quite nicely.

After a full-on year of study and research, I graduated in one of my new disciplines and took off for a celebratory week in NYC where my daughter was living.

That visit, when I moved naturally on my own merits into 'those' circles, meeting amazing people and creating mind-bogglingly fabulous new connections proved to be the catalyst for relocating to a new area and taking the leap into Interiors Therapy full time.

So my advice to you is, if you are currently wishing, hoping and praying for the right person to come into your life – stop it!

I'm not suggesting you take a year or even two out of the dating scene, all I'm saying is for a couple of months, rein in the need – no one likes needy anyway.

Instead, get on with enjoying life. Throw yourself into it with exuberance and happy abandon.

Want to go to a festival? Do it!

Want to get your teeth fixed? Call a dentist now while you don't have to kiss anyone with those funny sharp blocks on your teeth!

Want to change your hair, get a new hobby, lose some weight, gain some weight, laser your eyes, try go-karting, climb a mountain, master yoga, learn to scuba dive, write a book, experiment with veganism, get fillers, join a theatre group, become a film extra, travel the world with a backpack, become bilingual? Grab the new opportunities waiting for you right now. Don't imagine you have to be part of a couple before you can indulge in the sheer exhilaration of life.

If your friends try to hold you back, smile and get on with it! This isn't a mid-life crisis; this is you telling the world, *"Just bring it on!"*

Once you've got the hang of enjoying life as you want it to be, you'll inevitably become more attractive. Sorry peeps, that's just how it goes!

A couple of other suggestions you might like to consider will also change the way you see and think about yourself:

Dressing for the person you want to be

Are you still dressing as the person you were in that last disappointing relationship? No. Of course not, you are fresh, vibrant, irresistible and brimming with anticipation for what life is bringing you.

So this is the time to think about the person you really want to be. We've all heard the saying:

"Dress for the job you want, not the one you have."

I'm saying, do the same for your life.

Find out what suits you. Colours, styles, designs and stores. The places you used to shop in may not be the ones which will show you at your best now.

Push the boat out and try something new!

My wardrobe changed from office wear and jeans to a whirl of dance dresses, professional and practical clothes for Interiors Therapy and a selection of outfits for the various events, workshops and talks which are part of my life now.

As I knew I'd be travelling a lot, I also considered how much time I would have to think about laundry, packing and repacking between work engagements and whether I could afford to spend hours each week ironing as I had before (I can't!). That changed my perspective on fabrics and wardrobe basics, but I'm still a stranger to a capsule wardrobe – that is never going to happen!

You might find it interesting to ask a Colour Consultant to check the shades and seasons which work best for you. That certainly dealt with some of the more bizarre colour combinations I have worn in the past! Several of my clients have refined their wardrobes this way.

Much as I'd like to have the easy classic daytime style of Diane Keaton, or hold a stage dressed as elegantly as Audrey Hepburn, I'm an hourglass with a love of fine food and champagne and slightly shorter legs than the average! Once I embraced that I felt more comfortable in the clothes I wore. You can too.

Meditation/Hypnosis

My final energy shifter in this section is meditation. Now, full disclosure here, you are unlikely to find me in lotus on a cushion sitting in silence for hours on end. Nope. Maybe five minutes at the end of yoga if you push me and that's it! My mind starts chattering, and every bit of me is itching to be somewhere else.

So meditation for me had to be something non-intrusive and have the added bonus of making me switch off.

After trying a few guided meditations, I found my way to Dr Steve G Jones, clinical hypnotherapist. Most of his Hypnosis audios took the form of a guided meditation which very successfully put me to sleep. The added bonus was that I could choose from thousands of hypnosis tracks on everything from becoming more confident to igniting my kundalini energy (ooh er!).

Using the tracks regularly with a soft headphone headband to cover my eyes and my ears meant I slept very deeply and reprogrammed my brain without any effort whatsoever – result! I could even use it when I was sharing a room with friends, and it's brilliant on transatlantic flights.

So if sleep is still a challenge for you or you are retaining some limiting beliefs despite everything you've achieved so far, give hypnosis or guided meditation a try.

And if you have much more patience than me and want to join a meditation or mindfulness group – go for it!

You're now spiralling upwards with your energy and coming into the orbit of far more people. They are more likely to be on your wavelength than the person in the photo-shopped picture on Bumble, Match, Tinder, or wherever you happen to post your internet dating profile.

But before you jump in, I think it's time to prepare your Manifesto for Love™!

♥

CHAPTER 13

Why the Manifesto for Love™?

The concept of making a list of the desired qualities in a mate has been around in one form or another for centuries. Whether in the form of early humans selecting a strong, fast huntsman as a mate to ensure there was food in the cave, or royalty strategically marrying princes and princesses in nearby kingdoms to consolidate wealth or land.

Yes, those are extreme examples, but to all intents and purposes, not much has changed. Most people, whether they acknowledge it or otherwise, have a desired list of characteristics they want for their mate.

The thing is that for many amazing people, life, personal experience, parental interference, fate and numerous other factors have intervened to the point where they:

♥ tolerate unhappy relationships rather than be alone

♥ just settle for someone

- ❤ bounce from one unsatisfactory relationship to the next

- ❤ repeat the same relationship over and again with different people

- ❤ believe their last chance for love has gone

- ❤ accept a partner under family pressure

- ❤ stay in a controlling relationship because they are afraid to leave

- ❤ choose to be alone because it's easier that way

You might have experienced a number of those situations or just one. Whatever your circumstances, you are here now, dipping into this book and wondering whether this is going to be the catalyst to something better.

Relationship conditioning is changing as our world alters around us. Marriage is no longer the norm and has almost become a luxury Instagram status update for serial celebrity brides.

Cohabitation, sometimes within a few weeks of knowing a new partner, is often a means of sharing the bills rather than a declaration of love. Even after years of unwedded bliss with someone, it's simple to pack your things and walk away, leaving the debris of shattered dreams to impact on the rejected partner for years to come.

More people are choosing to live alone than ever before, and for those who can't afford to have their own home, a life as a lodger in the parental home or renting a shared space, with all of the restrictions that imposes, might be the only option.

So what does this rather bleak exposé of life in the 21st century have to do with Interiors Therapy and creating your Manifesto for Love™?

Well quite a lot actually – because by making you think about where you are now and what you really want in your life, we can work together to make it happen… and that's why you're really here.

CHAPTER 14

The Manifesto for Love™

Congratulations, you've made it at last! Your clutter has gone, your home and possessions are in harmony, and your environment is supporting you to move forward. You've taken control of your life, you look and feel amazing. You are your best self, and you are grateful, truly abundantly grateful, for the life you have right now.

Fantastic. Now you are in the right place to attract someone worthy of your love into your life.

Go back to the exercise you did in Chapter 2. Just have your answers to refer to. Those inner thoughts you had about yourself at the beginning of this book are likely to have altered along the way and while they won't all impact on the type of person you want in your life, some will.

So let's start with the basics, but first a cautionary tale about being specific. Do you remember I told you about my lovely friend Lynette, the first person to make a Manifesto for Love™ with me?

We were both new to this, the Manifesto for Love™ had worked for me, and I was a few months into my new relationship, but the concept hadn't been thoroughly road tested. Lynette made her Manifesto, stuck it up inside her wardrobe door and opened her heart and mind to meeting someone new.

Now Lynette had been extremely specific about a couple of things. Firstly, the man had to live within 5 miles of her home in a small country town. He had to be older than her and want children. Finally, he had to be keen on a very specific hobby which Lynette particularly enjoyed. I'm not going to name the sport, but trust me, its niche!

So picture the scene… Lynette has defined exactly what she is looking for. She's in her late 30s, very petite, still working towards her weight loss goals and she's on a mission. Lynette joined a dating site and searched on her criteria. One profile came up – just one!

After Lynette 'liked' the profile, she went dancing and was full of happy endorphins when she returned home to a message from the man inviting her out for a drink.

After they met at the local pub a few days later, Lynette was bursting with excitement. He was amazing, lived in the same town, wanted kids and marriage, shared the hobby (actually, not only did he share the hobby, he happened to be an expert in the field). They had talked until the pub closed, and then all the way back to her place when he walked her home.

"Why am I hearing a 'but'?" I asked her.

"Well, we missed one key thing off the Manifesto." she said.

"Uh huh, what was that?" I pricked up my ears, keen to learn where we had gone astray…

"His height," she replied, *"… he's 6'6."*

Oops, schoolgirl error!

So if there is something really important to you, like your partner being within a particular height, age or weight range, make sure you get specific on your Manifesto.

But, (and this is crucially important) never write your list with a particular individual in mind. Attempting to use your Manifesto for Love™ or implementing the Law of Attraction to interfere with the free-will of anyone else will distort the energy and rebound on you. Even if they are the right person for you, your attempt to dictate the outcome will backfire, and you might push them away permanently.

Your Manifesto for Love™ will draw the energy of a person with the attributes you desire and describe towards you. It can only do this if you make the Manifesto for Love™ when you are in a positive, balanced emotional state, and you can detach from the outcome and any specific person.

Now there might well be certain characteristics you have loved in previous partners, and you would like to experience those again with your new love… that's fine. If your ex was a fabulous cook and that's important to you, add 'great cook' to your Manifesto for Love™. Just don't attach that cooking ability to any particular person.

When I worked with Ahmed to define his Manifesto for Love™, he really struggled to put into words what he was looking for. He knew he wanted to be in a loving relationship but was unable to say what he was looking for. We talked about some of his previous girlfriends and what was wonderful about them. Then we translated that into positive statements to bring a new lady who combined all of those aspects into his life.

Other clients beginning the process are often already absolutely clear on what they don't want in a relationship. However, filling a list with 'don't want' statements is counter productive. The Law of Attraction doesn't notice the negative 'don't' or 'not' and will, therefore, work hard to bring you precisely the attributes you don't want. So reframe your negative statements into positive ones. For example, 'I don't want someone with bad teeth' could be transformed into 'they have healthy teeth and gums'.

Now you have a vague idea of what to include in your Manifesto for Love™, find something to write on and start creating your draft list. Sometimes it's fun to do this with trusted friends; for others, it's a very personal and deeply private exercise. Go with whatever works best for you.

This might feel a little like an interrogation of your deepest wishes, but believe me, having real clarity about your intentions is the best way to achieve a positive outcome.

These are some of the areas you might choose to include. They are purely a guide and if any of the aspects included below are irrelevant to you, simply ignore them. This is your list and yours alone.

Physical Characteristics

- ❤ Age range
- ❤ Height range
- ❤ Weight range
- ❤ Level of fitness
- ❤ Appearance – does it matter?
- ❤ Hair colour – do they even have hair?
- ❤ Teeth

Location

- ❤ How far are you willing to travel for a date?

- ❤ Do they live in a city, town or the country?

- ❤ Is their home easy to get to?

- ❤ Are you happy with a long-distance relationship?

Attitudes

- ❤ What are they like at home?

- ❤ How do they behave when you are out together?

- ❤ How they relate to his family and yours?

- ❤ Do they have lots of friends?

- ❤ Where do their friends fit into your life?

- ❤ Do their politics have to match yours? – does it matter?

Family situation

- ❤ Are they single, divorced, widowed, separated?

- ❤ Do they have children?

- ❤ Who do their children live with?

- ❤ Do they want children?

- ❤ How do they feel about your children?

- ❤ Do they have other family responsibilities?

Stage of life

- ❤ Are they employed? In education? Retired?

- ❤ Do they work for themselves?

- ❤ What sort of role do they have in life?

- ❤ What matters to them?

- ❤ Is their employment or status important to you?

Outlook on life

- ❤ What hobbies do they have?

- ❤ Are there particular sports which really matter to you?

- ❤ Do they have different hobbies or the same as yours?

- ❤ Is it important they are involved with your hobbies?

- ❤ What do they love to do for holidays?

- ❤ Do they relish travel? What sort?

- ❤ What sort of places do they like to stay in?

- ❤ Do they enjoy music?

- ❤ Is being in nature a good or bad thing?

- ❤ Is art, films, theatre or shows important? What sort?

- ❤ What radio station do they listen to?

- ❤ Is fashion or the way they dress important?

- ❤ What makes them laugh?

Background and culture:

- ❤ Is their religion or race important to you?

- ❤ Do they practice their religion?

- ❤ What is their attitude to your religion?

Values and beliefs:

- ❤ What motivates them?

- ❤ Honesty

- ❤ Loyalty

- ❤ Adventure

- ❤ Affection

- ❤ Community

- ❤ Competitiveness

- ❤ Creativity

- ❤ Economic security

- ❤ Effectiveness

- ❤ Energy

- ❤ Generosity

- ❤ Helping others

- ❤ Home

- ❤ Integrity

- ❤ Knowledge

- ❤ Openness

- ❤ Patience

- ❤ Pleasure

- ❤ Personal development

- ❤ Responsibility

- ❤ Self-respect

- ❤ Spirituality

- ❤ Spontaneity

- ❤ Success

- ❤ Time

- ❤ Truth

- ❤ Understanding

- ❤ Wisdom

Financial situation

- ❤ Do they need to have a particular income level?

- ❤ Do they need to own their own home?

- ❤ Are there trappings of wealth which are important to you?

- ❤ Does it matter if they earn less than you?

Things particularly important to you

- ❤ Do they need to drive, have a car?

- ❤ Are they fit and healthy? Does it matter?

- ❤ Are they vegan, vegetarian, carnivorous?

- ❤ How do they live?

- ❤ Are they tidy and house trained?

- ❤ Do they expect you to take care of them?

Once you've defined all of these areas – and while some will be important to you, others may not matter one jot – put them into one really positive list, by which I mean your statements must all be phrased in a positive way. This helps to focus your mind and activate the Law of Attraction.

To help you get the idea, these are some of the negative statements my clients have come up with, and the positive ways they have been rephrased for their Manifestos. Firstly, the women and then the men, although as you'll see many are interchangeable and some are quite revealing.

Ladies asked for:

No wigs	Has their own healthy hair
Does not snore	Sleeps quietly
Non-smoker	Has fresh breath and healthy lungs
Not a couch potato	Likes to exercise
Doesn't smell bad	Always smells good

Not lazy around the house	Tidy, neat and house trained
Doesn't sleep around	One-woman man
Doesn't lie to me	Honest and open
Doesn't dress badly	Looks good in clothes and without them
Expect me to always pay	Is financially comfortable and generous

Men asked for:

Hate loads of make-up	Is naturally attractive
Not high maintenance	Confident in who she really is
Mustn't try to change me	Loves me for who I am
Not insecure	Likes herself
Not money grabbing	Respects me financially
No stupidly high shoes	Always wears shoes she can walk in
Not social media obsessed	Respects boundaries on social media
No drama queens	Balanced and sees both sides

There are some statements I recommend everyone uses, although I suggest you put them into your own words:

Free and ready to love me

Emotionally available to me now and always

Fully aligned to allow our relationship to grow

Honest and truthful

Respectful of me, my interests and the people I love

Kind, caring and loyal

The right lover for me

Once you've finished, you will have created a list of positive statements about the person you want to share your life with. It's a way of fine-tuning the energy of that special someone so you, and the Universe, are absolutely clear about what you are looking for.

Before you rush to etch your Manifesto in stone, sit on it for a couple of days and then re-read it. Do you need to add anything else? Take something away? Be confident to add or remove if something important comes up. When it feels right, either type it and print it out, or write it out longhand on a piece of special paper.

Now place your Manifesto for Love™ in the relationship area of your home, your bedroom, or if you're a bit self-conscious about it, stick it on the inside of your wardrobe door.

Remember some of the statements on your Manifesto for Love™ will be ones you are willing to compromise on. You might be open to sharing your life with someone wonderful who is 5'8, although your Manifesto for Love™ says 5'9 - 6'2. Alternatively, your desire to meet someone with the same religion, cultural background or politics, a non-smoker or someone with their own teeth and hair might be non-negotiable. Inevitably other areas might be challenged as you shift your energy and start to meet amazing new people. That's what makes life fun!

Your Manifesto for Love™ gives you a blueprint you can refer to as you get to know someone. Just as a house is designed and built based on architectural drawings, your new relationship now has a sound foundation. You have really thought about what qualities and values you want in the person with whom you are inviting to share your life. The Manifesto for Love™ you have created is your personal key to the relationship door, unlocking and celebrating a potential partner's great qualities and simultaneously serving you as a red warning flag if they are falling short of the values and standards you desire.

CHAPTER 15

Using your Manifesto for Love™

Let's just be clear about one tiny point. Your Manifesto for Love™ is not going to be much use if you sit on your sofa watching TV and surfing the internet. A little more effort is required than swiping through dating sites on your phone.

Get out, smile more, chat to people, make eye contact. Practise being chatty and friendly with strangers, shop assistants, people in queues, even people who cold call you. Remember, a stranger is only a friend you haven't met yet. Express gratitude in a variety of ways. Hone your communication skills and find opportunities to make people smile. Play with Random Acts of Kindness to lift your energy from the mundane to the higher vibrational level, which allows you to manifest the things you want into your life.

Why am I suggesting this? What exactly has this got to do with your Manifesto for Love™? It's simple, when you spread good vibes your endorphins go up, you boost the energy around you, and this moves you to a higher vibrational level. It's from the highest vibrational level that you become magnetic, and when you are magnetic, it's so much easier to manifest anything and everything. This especially includes the energy of a person who matches your requirements.

Before I travelled to New York to spend time with my daughter, I reviewed my Manifesto for Love™. I had been dating someone who was heading in the right direction, but not quite the right one. I knew I had to fine-tune the age range I had written in my original Manifesto for Love™. I also wanted to include something about the potential partner having a good relationship with his family, as the guy I was dating was estranged from his children which felt really uncomfortable for me. This man wasn't right for me; I thanked him for some lovely dates and said goodbye.

So off I went to the Big Apple, clear on the energy of the man I was looking for and completely detached. To say I was magnetic was an understatement. We got special treatment in all sorts of ways – upgrades, business class travel, gifts, excellent tables, complimentary bottles of champagne, the best seats. I was turning heads (male and female) whenever I walked along the street and strangers were smiling and saying 'Hello' to me as we passed one another. Considering Manhattan isn't generally known for the friendliness of its residents; this was quite something! The thing was, it was all energetic. There was an 'indefinable something' drawing good stuff towards me, and it felt amazing.

It went on for the entire time in New York. When I boarded my flight home, the magic was still in full force. The man in the next seat and I talked all night. It was unexpected, delightful and very powerful. He checked almost all of the criteria on my Manifesto for Love™, and we dated for a while afterwards. Drawing him into my life proved I could be absolutely clear about the attributes of the person I want to share my life with, and that there really are men in the world who combine every one of those attributes and more!

The only tiny fly in the ointment was that he was recently divorced and wasn't emotionally available. That's why my Manifesto for Love™ now says 'Emotionally available to me now and always.' I am abundantly grateful for the experience of getting to know Airplane Man.

So does the Manifesto for Love™ work straight away?

It would be more accurate to say the Manifesto for Love™ starts working in your best interests straight away. Now this might mean the person you've fancied for ages suddenly hooks up with someone else and disappears out of your life. That will have happened because they don't fit your energetic criteria (no matter how much you want to believe they do!).

Your Manifesto for Love™ will draw the energy of the type of people you would like to date into your sphere, but you have to invest a little effort into making that happen. Get out and talk to people, put yourself in places they might frequent and show up as the person you want to be.

People who fit the bill can turn up in the most unexpected places, and if you aren't open to the possibility, the ideal romantic partner for you could walk straight past unnoticed.

With a Manifesto for Love™, as you get to know someone, you can check in with your Manifesto and see how they measure up. If after a couple of dates their values, attributes and beliefs are not chiming with yours, then you can walk away in the knowledge that this was not a good long-term love match, fine tune your Manifesto for Love™ if you need to, and move on.

Set standards of respect, consideration and love which you choose not to compromise on. It saves a great deal of heartache down the line.

When the right person does waltz into your life, and you embark on a relationship together, please do yourself an enormous favour and re-read Chapter 12 to consciously keep your vibration at a high magnetic level. It's well known that the first heady days and weeks of a new relationship send all sorts of happy chemicals coursing through our bodies. It's hard to think about anyone other than that 'special someone'.

Falling in love leaves you vulnerable. If they don't call when they say they will, or unavoidably miss a date or misunderstand a text, it's easy to over-analyse or assume something is wrong. This is a crucial time to keep your vibrational level high. Stay magnetic, keep doing your thing with your friends, at home and at work. Be yourself, think about things other than the love interest and allow the relationship to develop from a balanced and happy place.

You were in magnetic flow before you met them, and they were attracted into your life because you were absolutely clear on the person you wanted, and your energy matched theirs in the most beautiful and compelling way. The Law of Attraction manifested them into your energy when you were in your best place, so it's crucial to stay there. At this point, when you may be feeling love, desire and anticipation of a future together tipping you over the edge of reason, by maintaining your high vibrational level it helps you avoid the neediness, vulnerability and sleepless nights which often come with falling in love.

I have seen wonderful people change their vibe from blissful anticipation to a place of powerlessness when they fall hard for someone. By believing one individual is the key to your emotions and your entire future, you give someone else power over your emotions. If you sink into a pit of irrational despondency, chase them and build your dreams and expectations about a future with them, you are building on foundations which are no more stable than sand on a beach. The energy between you won't be in harmony anymore, and even the most perfect of partners can disappear, leaving you questioning everything about yourself.

A relationship grows based on balance and respect. Love at first sight does happen, and yet if you don't keep your energy high, it can burn out as suddenly and permanently as a firework at New Year, leaving you confused and wondering what just happened.

When 'love at first sight' does survive, it can grow into something long term and really special. This happens because both parties give the relationship equal energy. However, this level of love cannot grow if one person is pushing their energy too hard in the direction of the other, because, as you might remember from very basic physics, specifically Newton's third law:

For every action, there is an equal and opposite reaction.

Sir Isaac Newton

Essentially, putting this into relationship terms, the more energy you push towards someone, the further you push them away.

So balance in any relationship, right from the start, is key to its success. If you have been in a situation where someone was overwhelming you with messages, calls, or wanting to be with you all the time and your response was to back off completely, then you have experienced Newton's third law.

Those calls and messages were energy at a definable level – you could see and read them, and it felt uncomfortable to you. Put simply, their energy was too much, and it repelled you. If you had been responding at the same level, with the same energetic force, then there would have been balance between you, and it would have felt very much more comfortable.

Right back in Chapter 4, I explained that we are all energy. Every one of us is made up of a complex feast of energetic particles; protons, photons, atoms, neurons (and within those, quarks) and goodness knows what other hidden treats waiting to be identified by science. We can't see any of these energies, but they are inside us, around us and impact on every part of our lives and experience.

This invisible energy creates a direct link between you and the person you are connecting with. It has an impact, arguably a much greater impact, than anything you can observe at face value.

So, if you are obsessing about 'the one', talking about them all the time, waiting for them to message you, scrutinising their social media, analysing every contact, checking your astrological compatibility, numerology, Chinese horoscope and imagining all sorts of ways of connecting with them (sound familiar?); then your invisible energy is bombarding the object of your affection with a full on air-raid. They might not realise it's you, but they feel unsettled by the energetic sensation. Scary huh? It's the energetic equivalent of obsessive stalking, and believe me, their subconscious will feel it.

Now, if they feel the same way about you, they will respond in a way which lets you know. You'll get the attention you hope for; they will want to text, talk, meet and be around you. However, if they don't share the intensity of desire or affection for you, or your energy hits them at a time when they need to focus elsewhere, then your thoughts will push them away. It will happen so quickly that what seemed initially to be 'written in the stars', will fizzle out faster than the bubbles in a cheap bottle of champagne.

If this person is the one for you, your vibe has to stay at peak performance level to draw the best of everything into your life. Take responsibility for your energy, expend it wisely and keep lots back for yourself.

If the object of your affections pulls back, recover your energy quickly. It's so tempting to keep pushing it out towards them — don't. Just don't!

I've heard so many tales of woe on this subject, and frankly have made this mistake so many times in my own life. When I see and hear my friends and clients talking endlessly about someone they have feelings for and that person has either ended things, withdrawn or even disappeared without explanation, I know it's because the situation has been over-energised with comments like:

I know it's meant to be; I just have to be sure she realises it too.

All the stars aligned, so we met, but now he's gone quiet…

I messaged him two days ago, and he hasn't responded…

Everything was going so well, and then it just stopped…

She hasn't done what she said she would…

I know she's read my WhatsApp, why doesn't she respond?

I feel desperate when I don't hear from him.

I'm so angry she hasn't returned my calls or texts.

I think about him all the time; I can't focus on anything else.

I don't understand why…

They must be confused because …

I'm really hurt by their behaviour

I have to know what's going on.

My advice is always to reframe your thinking as soon as you realise you are behaving this way. The sleepless nights are not worth it! Absolutely, deliberately, without question, pull back your power and focus on something other than that one individual. Find something else to do or think about, anything which doesn't give you headspace to focus on them. By withdrawing your energy, you give them space to realise what you represent to them, and if they come back, then you can then respond at their energetic level, and learn a valuable lesson along the way. Always use your energy with integrity.

The thing is though, if you have overwhelmed them before you reframe your thinking, it's probably too late. You will have pushed them too far, and effectively scared them away. You have to be balanced, aware and considered about the energy you put out from the very beginning. Sending out a flaming ball of passionate, hurt, needy, angry or desperate energy towards an individual you are getting to know is going to overpower them unless they have the same level of feeling for you.

You are the only one who can dictate how you think and feel right now and ensure that you are putting a balanced level of energy into growing a new relationship and into your happy future together.

♥

CHAPTER 16

Conclusion

So there you have it, Interiors Therapy for Love, and much more.

At the beginning of the book, I explained Interiors Therapy is a process and the results you achieve are directly commensurate with the effort you put in.

By following each stage through to completion before moving on to the next you will, without a doubt, experience change, new opportunities, unexpected delights and put yourself in the strongest position to meet the sort of person with whom you can enjoy a happy, fulfilling, love relationship, or find new delight in the one you already enjoy.

Along the way, you may well find unhelpful people or situations leave your life or something major happens to jolt you out of the rut you've been in. Sometimes this can be painful and leave you feeling rootless or lost. Please trust that everything really is happening for a reason, and that it's all in your best interests, no matter how much it hurts right now. In a couple of years, when you look back, you'll realise if it hadn't been this way, you couldn't or wouldn't have taken the next steps which were essential to you meeting the right person or achieving your desire.

In the meantime, for hints, tips, guidance and access to experienced Interiors Therapy experts, you are welcome to join the Facebook group www.facebook.com/interiorstherapy We would love to see you there to share the wins and achievements you experience along the way.

Enjoy the journey and reap the rewards of making Interiors Therapy your new lifestyle choice.

Suzanne

CHAPTER 17

Useful hints

Use these simple energy boosts for your home to help you maintain the great vibe, avoid returning to old patterns of stagnation and keep you focused on creating and maintaining the life you love.

Space clear every few months to keep the energy sparkling

The change of season is a natural time for this, as is New Year or the Chinese New Year, but do it when it works for you. If something sad or traumatic happens, as soon as you are able, refresh the energy of your home.

Stay on top of domestic clutter

Catch yourself if you start to notice clutter creeping back. Notice where you are putting it and review that area of your life to see what's going on.

Be open to new ways to enjoy and streamline your life

As you get more in tune with your home and your life, you'll become aware of ways you can make it easier or more fun. Take new opportunities, say 'yes' more than 'no', and make the most of the additional time and experiences you gain.

Clutter catcher

At Christmas and on birthdays have a dedicated box into which all family members put the gifts which they have received but do not want to keep. This is a 'zero recriminations' space. If there is something in the box you truly desire, then liberate it for your own use. Otherwise, the box is donated to a charity so the unloved items can find new homes where they will be appreciated.

Sale Shopping

If there is a particularly expensive item you're longing to buy and you're holding out to get a reduction in the sale, that's great. Go right ahead.

But if you go sale shopping out of habit, remember all those clothes, shoes, furniture etc. are still there and marked down because no one else wanted them. Those scented candles might smell a bit peculiar. The gift sets aren't necessarily going to give you what you want, and that games console may be obsolete in a month.

Working with clients, 99% of them have clothes hanging up still carrying the sale label. It could be months or years since they were bought, but they remain unworn. Seriously, if you buy something, do so with the expectation of wearing it straight away, and if that's not going to happen, don't buy it.

Please never buy in anticipation of losing a dress size, or purchase shoes which are designer and 50% off, but are slightly too large so you can't actually walk in them. Be more considered in your sale shopping habits, think about the story decorative items are telling, and stop clutter before it even reaches your home.

One of the things which my clients say is that after Interiors Therapy they become a lot more circumspect about shopping.

"I hate you," wrote Marisa in a tongue-in-cheek email between Christmas and New Year.

"I used to do the Boxing Day sales, spend a fortune and come back really frazzled after buying a load of stuff I never wore. Since the Interiors Therapy, I wasn't even tempted. You've ruined my shopping habit for me! I stayed home with my husband and the kids. We watched a movie and laughed together for hours. I feel truly blessed."

LINKS

Contact Suzanne Roynon

International Interiors Therapist, Speaker and Coach

1:1 appointments are available in the UK and Europe

Video appointments internationally by arrangement

www.interiorstherapy.com

www.facebook.com/interiorstherapy

REFERENCES

Chapter 1

Julia Roberts, *Pretty Woman*, 1990
Miia Koponen, Dating Coach and Matchmaker
www.miiakoponen.com/

Chapter 3

Jim Rohn, Motivational Speaker
https://www.jimrohn.com/

David Burkus, Author and Speaker
https://davidburkus.com/

Chapter 5

Karen Kingston
www.spaceclearing.com/web

Clear Your Clutter with Feng Shui
Creating Sacred Space with Feng Shui

Fiona Harrold
https://www.fionaharrold.com/

Ceroc
www.ceroc.com

Chapter 7

Marie Kondo
https://konmari.com/
The Life Changing Magic of Tidying Up

Vanessa Edwards
www.vandaehworks.co.uk/

Alison Knox
www.everydayangelsart.com

William Spear
Feng Shui Made Easy

Part II

Lyric: *These Foolish Things*
Holt Marvell & Jack Strachey
I like the Bryan Ferry version best

Part III

Chapter 11

Mrs Hinch Instagram @MrsHinchHome
Or search on YouTube for Sophie Hinch

Chapter 13

Dr Steve G Jones, Clinical Hypnotherapist
www.stevegjones.com

www.betterlivingwithhypnosis.net

ABOUT THE AUTHOR

Photo: Frances Newman Photography

Suzanne Roynon is 'The UK's leading Interiors Therapist'

Suzanne is a speaker, author and clutter-free coach based in Hertfordshire, UK. In 2019, national newspaper features about her powerful new Interiors Therapy method explained how a home could be a 'Manrepeller' or 'Womanrepeller' preventing the occupant from enjoying a healthy, balanced, loving relationship. The articles became click-bait worldwide, generating media interest, interviews and an international client base. The need for Interiors Therapy in hundreds of thousands of homes became abundantly clear.

Combining 20 years of practical experience, coaching, energy therapies and a sprinkling of Feng Shui, Interiors Therapy is a dynamic five-step process developed by Suzanne to achieve clarity about the impact of possessions, clear stagnation, create transformation, invite a flow of new opportunities and maximise the Law of Attraction.

In the final section *of Welcome Home – how stuff makes or breaks your relationship,* Suzanne reveals how to create your Manifesto for Love™. For the first time in print, Suzanne describes a technique previously reserved for VIP clients. She emphasises firm foundations are essential for this potent step and warns readers to write their Manifesto only after the successful completion of Interiors Therapy in the home.

In addition to speaking and teaching, Suzanne delivers an online Interiors Therapy Masterclass programme. She offers one-to-one consultations for clients in the UK and Europe and by video further afield. Find out more at www.interiorstherapy.com and join the Facebook community for updates and inspiration https://www.facebook.com/interiorstherapy

Notes:

Notes:

Notes:

Notes:

Notes: